From Trainee to Teacher

# From Trainee to Teacher
## Reflective Practice for Novice Teachers

Thomas S.C. Farrell

SHEFFIELD UK   BRISTOL CT

Published by Equinox Publishing Ltd.

UK:    Office 415, The Workstation, 15 Paternoster Row, Sheffield, South
       Yorkshire S1 2BX
USA:   ISD, 70 Enterprise Drive, Bristol, CT06010

www.equinoxpub.com

First published 2016



British Library Cataloguing-in-Publication Data

A catalogue record for this book is available from the British Library.

ISBN-13    978 1 84553 150 8  (hardback)
           978 1 84553 195 9  (paperback)

Library of Congress Cataloging-in-Publication Data

Names: Farrell, Thomas S. C. (Thomas Sylvester Charles), author.
Title: From trainee to teacher : reflective practice for novice teachers /
   Thomas S.C. Farrell.
Description: Sheffield, UK ; Bristol, CT : Equinox Pub. Ltd, 2016. |
Includes
   bibliographical references and index.
Identifiers: LCCN 2015031236 | ISBN 9781845531508 (hb) | ISBN 9781845531959 (pb)
Subjects: LCSH: First year teachers–Handbooks, manuals, etc. | English
   language–Study and teaching–Foreign speakers–Handbooks, manuals, etc.
Classification: LCC LB2844.1.N4 F37 2016 | DDC 371.14/4–dc23
LC record available at http://lccn.loc.gov/2015031236

Typeset by S.J.I. Services, New Delhi
Printed and bound by Lightning Source Inc. (La Vergne, TN), Lightning Source UK Ltd. (Milton Keynes), Lightning Source AU Pty. (Scoresby, Victoria).

# Contents

# Chapter 1

# Teaching: A Profession That Eats Its Young

## Preamble

In the ensuing pages of this book you will read about the first-year teaching experiences of three novice ESL (English as a second language) teachers in Canada. I begin the book by immediately divulging some excerpts that will be discussed in more detail in later chapters, because I want to set the scene, an alarming one really, of what is happening in silence in our profession in terms of how we abandon our graduates when they enter real classrooms for the first time. So here is a "sneak peek" of what is to come ....

The big day has finally arrived. All three ESL novice teachers said that they were very excited to begin their careers and could not wait for their first day. They arrived at the school and walked in, and then the confusion commenced. All three said that they immediately felt they were not part of the school or part of the teaching team that already existed in the school. T3 noted: "It's not welcoming." After that she felt she was "thrown in to survive yourself." T2 recalled that on the first day she was not introduced to anyone in the school when she arrived; she remarked, "none of us were introduced." When she finally entered a classroom with students, T3 said that her initial shock was the large size of the class. She reflected: "I think I just had no clue about the class size because I was expecting to work with 10 or 12 students and it didn't occur to me that it would be 24 or 25. Oh wow, this is a lot of people." T3 summed up all three novice teachers' realizations of their first week on the job: "We're into the deep water now, and it is kind of sink or swim." Yes, sink or swim is a worrying comment from these novice teachers, made in their first week on the job, and so it seems that TESOL (teaching English to speakers of other languages), like the larger profession of teaching, eats its young. However, as you continue reading this book you will see how, although at many times these teachers seemed to be sinking, they were able to keep afloat as they navigated their first semester. This was largely thanks to the help of an informal teacher reflection group, as described in greater detail in subsequent chapters. I believe as you read this book you may wonder whether they would have survived had it not been for the regular group discussions in the novice ESL teacher reflection group. I leave this to each individual reader to reflect on. Perhaps the contents of this book may lead you to conclude that TESOL is a profession that eats its young. One thing for sure I realize from writing this book is that the contents are a wake-up call for the TESOL profession as a whole.

## Introduction

Teaching is "the profession that eats its young" (Halford, 1998: 34). This is a statement widely recognized in the literature on general education. Some of the numbers are astonishing: the overall average career length of a teacher (any teacher) in the U.S. is eleven years (Belmonte, 2006). This is similar to the career length of a professional athlete who must endure the demands of a physical sport and all that it entails, with injuries and so on. In addition, some 30 per cent of all teachers leave the field within their first three years; and it gets worse, because within five years, nearly half of all novice teachers leave their jobs (Ingersoll & Smith, 2003). Some have even compared the teaching profession to a revolving door (U.S. Department of Education, 2000). Although anecdotal evidence suggests that this may also be true for the TESOL profession, it is not much talked about by language teacher educators. This is mostly because there is little agreement about what constitutes the knowledge base of the profession: language teacher education programs vary greatly both in length (from a weekend course to an MA degree) and in content, with some focusing exclusively on theory (such as second language acquisition theory or linguistics) and very few concerned with how teachers can put into practice what they have learned in these programs.

Yes, saying TESOL is a profession that eats its young is a dramatic statement, but reading the preamble above has given you a foretaste that it is a statement which has some reality for some novice ESL teachers. Indeed, some teachers have such a bad experience at the beginning of their careers that they decide in their very first week to leave the profession, feeling that their choice of vocation has been a mistake. Thus, many novice teachers, once so inspired to "change lives" (a comment from a novice teacher), just drift away before they can make a difference. As language teacher educators we must look both within and beyond our programs and ask ourselves: Are we actually preparing novice teachers for the reality of real classrooms? We must ask ourselves how we teacher educators can make a difference to the lives of novice teachers by some intervention that can help them through the difficult transition into real classrooms. I hope the contents of this book will offer some ideas, especially chapters 9 and 10. But first we must ask some hard questions.

## Why the Revolving Door?

So what is happening here and why this revolving door? After all, many teacher educators, teachers, students, administrators, and even novice teachers themselves assume that once novice teachers have graduated from their education courses they will be able to apply what they have learned during their first year of teaching. Why shouldn't they, the argument goes, surely the contents of the teacher education programs would be of direct help to the novice teachers in their first year, similar to, say, courses in medical training. When students graduate from medical school they are able to use what they have learned in their practice—at least one would imagine and hope so, if one is to follow a young doctor's orders. (In fact, most people do not question what the doctor orders, out of respect for the profession or out of fear of ill health).

However, in the TESOL profession it is often the case that once novice teachers get into a real classroom and must interact with real colleagues in a real school, the ideals, aspirations and, yes, the hopes that they have formed during their teacher education programs are often replaced (some say "washed away") by the realities of the social and political contexts of the school (Freeman, 1994). Unfortunately many novice teachers are often at a loss about what to do and most times are left alone (the teacher education programs that they graduated from have abandoned them) to navigate such a treacherous and difficult journey towards full socialization into the profession. Several of them do not make it.

There are many reasons for this, as noted above, such as a disconnect between the content of teacher education programs and the reality of an ESL teacher's life, when viewed from the perspective of teacher training, and chapter 9 provides some ideas on how this can be partially rectified. In addition, when looked at in the school setting, there are disconnects evident in how novice teachers are being socialized (or not) into the profession, and chapter 10 will outline some suggestions on how this situation too may be improved. One immediate issue is the fact is that when novice teachers begin their career they have to perform all the same activities as the most experienced teachers in the school from their very first day. As Redman (2006: xii) has pointed out, "The teacher is responsible for the nuts and bolts of managing the classroom, developing effective lesson plans ... addressing the standards, taking roll ... collaborating with colleagues. The list is endless."

However, unlike most experienced teachers, novice teachers have not yet built up the repertoire of skills required to accomplish all of this, and will need help in dealing with these multiple tasks from their very first day on the job. Of course, a few schools have some kind of induction program which may include the appointment of a mentor to help novice teachers through their first year, but in the TESOL profession, anecdotal evidence suggests this is the exception rather than the rule as many language schools are in the business of making money and cannot "afford" to appoint such a person (as mentor) which will take away from teaching time. Such was the case for the three novice ESL teachers reported on in this book.

As a result of the failings of teacher education programs and the schools in which teachers are placed in their first year, some novice teachers not only feel that they have not been prepared adequately for teaching but also become so disillusioned that they begin to reconsider their career choice. Unfortunately, some novice teachers decide there and then that they may have made an incorrect decision (because of all their negative experiences) and ultimately leave the profession at a great loss to everyone, not to mention the disillusioned teachers themselves. As Peterson & Williams (1998: 730) have noted: "the quality of the first teaching experience is more important in retaining new teachers than either the quality of the teacher preparation program or the new teacher's prior academic performance."

## The First Year in TESOL

A lot of the research that I have reported on so far has discussed the first year of teaching in the field of general education with only some references to the field of TESOL. I have noted that a lot of studies have found that many novice teachers who experience a bad beginning to their careers may consider leaving in their first year without ever having known the joys of teaching that many experienced teachers have come to appreciate over the years. In the TESOL profession, too, we can ask similar questions as were asked in the field of general education:

- What happens to novice teachers once they complete the many diploma, certificate, undergraduate and graduate programs, and do they too experience any negative events during their first years?
- How are first-year TESOL teachers socialized into the profession?
- What issues do they face in their first year?
- How has their teacher education program prepared them for their first year? What kinds of induction programs exist in TESOL schools?

The list of questions we can ask goes on, yet the shocking truth is that we in TESOL do not know much about what novice teachers experience in their first year, beyond a few studies. Among those that do exist, some in particular (Richards, 1998; Farrell, 2003, 2006) are important because they report on the socialization and development of novice English language teachers in their first year in different international settings, and also provide useful implications for second language teacher education programs that to my knowledge have not yet been applied.

Richards (1998), using a combination of questionnaires, classroom observations and analysis of discussions during monthly teacher meetings, discovered that when novice teachers graduated from a teacher preparation program in Hong Kong their primary concerns during their first year of teaching were to establish a relationship with their students, and to cover the prescribed curriculum. Furthermore, Richards (1998: 186) observed that these first-year teachers seemed to completely abandon or ignore many of the principles from their teacher education program that were "regarded as central to second language teaching." He concluded that, among other reasons, the context may have played an influential role in the teachers' preferences for "familiar routines and practices," rather than trying new approaches they had learned in the teacher education program (ibid.: 187). As a result of his findings, Richards proposed that teacher education should "explicitly align itself with local practices or ... work to change those practices" (ibid.: 190).

Farrell (2003, 2006) detailed a case study of how a first-year English language teacher in Singapore balanced a delicate, and sometimes conflicting, role between learning to teach and learning to become a teacher within an established school culture in Singapore. In the later study (2006), Farrell used narrative and descriptive data from his earlier study (2003) and superimposed a *story structure framework*, that followed a pattern of setting—complication—resolution. The purpose of the framework was to impose some order on the experiences of the first-year teacher and thus attempt to give them coherence so they could be examined by the novice teacher in the study, as well as by other novice teachers and language teacher educators. The analysis revealed that the novice teacher faced three main complications during his first year: his learner-centered approach to teaching (derived from his teacher education program) versus the school's established teacher-centered approach; the conflict between the novice teacher's desired curriculum and the school's required curriculum; and various complications related to collegial relations.

Farrell (2009) suggested that teacher education programs introduce specific courses dedicated to first-year teaching and that there should be more communication between teacher education programs and schools. The first approach addresses the issues of transition raised above by making direct linkages to teaching in the first year in teacher preparation courses. While some language teacher educators may well include such references in their individual courses, currently there seem to be few courses devoted explicitly to this area. An alternative to this current hit-or-miss approach, Farrell (2009) notes, would be the addition of a course, perhaps entitled "Teaching in the first year," which deals directly with the experiences, challenges and needs associated with novice teaching. As Farrell (2006) suggests, course content might include the development of skills in anticipatory reflection where novice teachers have opportunities to discuss and thus become more aware of what the transition from the teacher education program to the real world of the classroom might mean. Specific activities could involve analysis of written case studies from different contexts (see Farrell, 2008 for more on this) that follow the story structure framework outlined in Farrell's 2006 study.

Farrell (2009) advocates that teachers in preparation could also be asked to create a profile of the school in which they intend to teach, discuss their teaching issues with the current teachers and observe classes (a sort of "apprenticeship of observation"), before they take up full-time employment. Where this is not possible, practicing language teachers could be invited as guest speakers to discuss and respond to questions of practice, or videos of classroom practice could be used for analysis of various teaching approaches. Further, as suggested earlier by Farrell (1999), language educators could give pre-service teachers reflective assignments that assist them to unlock and articulate prior beliefs about language learning and teaching, some of which may be the result of the "apprenticeship of observation" mentioned above. In this way, novice second language teachers can become more aware of the origins of their underlying beliefs and how they can influence the approaches to learning and teaching they adopt during their first year.

The second approach Farrell (2009) talked about involves building school—teacher educator partnerships. He suggested that with a reduced teaching load, and the assistance of teacher educator mentors, novice second language teachers would have time to absorb and reflect on the various challenges they face during their first year as teachers. Unfortunately, anecdotal evidence from teachers in their first years, and findings from the limited number of research studies that have been conducted, suggest that these issues are not adequately addressed in language teacher education programs. In addition, not many programs have implemented any of these suggestions, so novice teachers are still leaving the TESOL profession because they feel they have not been prepared adequately for their first year of teaching. As pointed out earlier, they are left to their own devices to navigate this difficult transition from the teacher education program to the first year of teaching and many do not make it. I also mentioned that there are not many detailed accounts of what really happens to novice ESL teachers in their first year. This book is one attempt at adding to the knowledge on the experiences of novices in the TESOL profession.

## Outline of the Book

This chapter has made the case for the importance of focusing on novice teachers, as we are a profession that tends to eat our young. It has outlined the situation regarding the lack of information about what novice ESL teachers actually experience during their first year and has laid the way for the subsequent chapters that report on the experiences of a group of three novice ESL teachers in Canada during their first year.

As no in-depth case study of novice ESL teacher experiences in their first year of teaching has been accounted for in the TESOL literature, chapter 2 discusses in detail how data for this study were gathered and analyzed, and outlines the overall framework that guided the research on the three novice ESL teachers reported in subsequent chapters. This chapter also sets the scene for the novice teacher reflection group by describing the overall interpersonal climate of all the group discussions, before going into the particular topics they talked about as narrated in detail in subsequent chapters. These topics are not presented in order of their frequency but rather in chronological order as experienced by the teachers themselves.

Chapter 3 outlines and discusses the transition novice teachers must make from their teacher education programs to the first year in real contexts. The chapter reports the shock that many experience with this transition and the challenges they must face in real classrooms and interacting with new colleagues. The chapter points out that many novice ESL teachers report that they feel they have not been prepared adequately for this reality, basically because the TESOL profession does not know what novice teachers actually experience during their transition.

Chapter 4 discusses the initial transition shocks all three novice ESL teachers reported that they experienced from their very first day on the job, and especially notes that they were given no orientation or induction when they arrived. In addition the chapter records that the novice teachers did not have any mentor appointed to guide them and they did not know whom to go to for information or feedback in those first few weeks. As they realized they were on their own they were compelled to learn for themselves what they needed to do in order to survive in their classroom and with their colleagues.

Chapter 5 explores what the teachers talked about at the group meetings. This includes the actual teaching approaches and methods they used in their practice, and what they know or believe about these approaches and methods. The chapter also talks about the impact of the school context (in particular the administration) on their teaching, such as the need to produce weekly lesson plans for a prescribed curriculum. Also outlined in the chapter are the novice teachers' views on what works and what does not work in their lessons and how to deal with issues related to classroom management.

Chapter 6 discusses how they evaluated their teaching. More specifically the chapter outlines what they talked about in terms of effective lesson plans and how these played out in their classrooms—that is, how well an approach, a method, the lessons/classes and the course were progressing. These discussions also included their perceptions of their learners' responses and behaviors, as well as student perceptions and opinions of the class.

Chapter 7 explores the novice teachers' perceptions of their role identities during their first semester, and discusses which of these may have been assigned by others and which they have taken on themselves. Reflecting on teacher role identity allows language educators a useful lens into the *who* of teaching and how teachers construct and reconstruct their views of themselves and their roles as language teachers in relation to their peers and in their classroom context. The chapter outlines and discusses thirteen professional role identities that emerged from the reflective sessions, grouped into clusters under the three main roles.

Following on from this, chapter 8 explores the perceptions of all three novice ESL teachers about teaching style, based on an analysis of all the transcripts of the group meetings. Teaching style reflects the teacher's values and beliefs, which are reflected in how a teacher acts during the teaching and learning process in a classroom. The chapter outlines and discusses how each of the three novices' teaching styles is influenced by her personality, her experience of what works best, her teaching methods and by established practice.

Chapter 9 discusses how novice ESL teachers can be empowered through the use of reflective practice both in teacher education programs (the focus of the chapter) and during their first year (the focus of the following chapter). Specifically, the chapter outlines in detail how novice teachers can receive instruction in how to engage in systematic and structured reflection on practice using a framework that has five stages or levels: philosophy of practice, principles of practice, theory of practice, actual practice and beyond practice.

Chapter 10 follows on by discussing how novice teachers can continue their reflections in their first year, which becomes especially important if they have no real induction program or mentor support and, as a result, are left to sink or swim. The chapter points out that teacher reflection groups can help novice ESL teachers through this challenging transition/praxis shock from the teacher education program to the first year of teaching, so that they will swim and not sink.

## The Aim of This Book

I hope the report and analysis of the experiences of the three novice ESL teachers presented in this book will have some benefits (financial as well as educational) for language teacher education programs, ministries involved in such education programs and school administrators/boards that employ newly qualified teachers, and most importantly for novice teachers themselves. Vast amounts of funds are used to train ESL teachers each year. These are spent not only on instructing them in theory but also on pre-service placement during the period of their practicum. Indeed, the high rates of novice teacher attrition create a significant economic strain on provincial and educational budgets (Ingersoll & Smith, 2003). Yes, we can train new teachers but all this training costs enormous amounts of money, which is lost in the case of teachers who leave the profession so early. So it is better to *retain* ESL teachers rather than spend excessively to train new teachers every year.

The findings of this research will lead to greater awareness of the needs of novice ESL teachers in their first year, from their perspective. One only has to look at the titles of the chapters in this book in order to see that all is not well in our profession and that novice teachers are suffering (going by the experiences of the three who feature here): *A Profession That Eats Its Young*, *"Forget All You Learned at___,"* *Transition Shock*, *"The First Week Is Like You're in a Swamp," "Here's the Book, Go Teach," "It Was Very Dry," "I Want To Be Me"* and *"You Put Your Personal Stamp on It."* Each of these chapters has presented the various issues, challenges and adjustments these three novice teachers had to make in order to remain afloat. They were basically left alone throughout the process and had to navigate their first semester without much guidance; at times felt they were swimming frantically just so that they would not submerge. Yes, all three novice ESL teachers were on part-time contracts, and the administration may have decided not to make any investment in them as their future status at that school was uncertain. However, what is ironic is that each novice teacher at that school had to begin on such a contract with the hope of getting a more stable full-time contract in the future. Who knows, perhaps the administration had a Darwinian policy of accepting only those who survived this rough period of apprenticeship. Of course, what is needed is more care for the correct socialization of novice ESL teachers. As Johnson (1996: 48) correctly proposed, the process should be "less like 'hazing' and more like professional development."

I hope that the knowledge gained from reading about our three novice ESL teachers will be of help to educators in answering the important question: Why do so many beginning teachers leave the teaching profession? Such knowledge should be fed back in language teacher education and development programs so that ESL teachers can be better prepared for the realities of challenges they may face in the first year of teaching. Indeed, as Freeman (1994) cautioned language educators and novice teachers alike, what is presented in language teacher education programs may be completely washed away by the first-year experiences. So from an educational perspective the main beneficiaries of this book should be novice ESL teachers, second language educators and school administrators—because all three have major stakes in the successful induction of first-year ESL teachers. The findings of the study can help all three educational stakeholders to come together and work in collaboration to make for a smooth transition for novice ESL teachers from their second language teacher preparation programs to their first year(s) of teaching. The idea is that the knowledge garnered from the research presented here can be used to better inform special language teacher educators/programs so that novice teachers can be better prepared for the complexity of real classrooms.

## How to Use This Book

*From Trainee to Teacher: Reflective Practice for Novice Teachers* is intended to be a companion for all novice ESL teachers because it provides commentary and guidance directly related to the experiences of three of their colleagues during their first year. This book is also for teacher educators, and program administrators and supervisors who are responsible for providing professional development opportunities for novice ESL teachers; and for those taking graduate courses in TESOL who are interested in the field of second language teacher education The book is written in a clear and accessible style and assumes no previous background in teacher education.

In addition, each chapter includes **Reflective Breaks** that prepare the reader to reflect on issues discussed in the chapter and consider how these may be relevant to his/her particular context. Indeed, novice teachers can gather as a group to reflect on the various topics discussed by the novice ESL teachers in this book, and consider the importance of these topics in relation to their context. They can use these topics as a means of generating reflection in their own particular settings and then compare their findings with those reported in this book.

## Conclusion

This chapter has pointed out that the research in general education studies has revealed that many teachers leave the profession in their first year because of the mostly negative experiences they face during this novice year. The numbers reveal that even if there is some form of an induction program for novice teachers, they still feel burdened with the demands of what they must face inside and outside the classroom while they are still in the process of learning how to teach. In fact, they are expected to do exactly what the most experienced teachers do, and get no time or space to reflect on what is really happening and how to handle it. What is most shocking for the TESOL profession is that too few studies have actually paid attention to what happens to first-year ESL teachers on the job and we still have a huge disconnect between the theories offered in teacher education courses and the reality of what novice teachers experience. The chapter has introduced the idea of forming a novice ESL teacher reflection group in order to document these teachers' actual experiences so that we can learn more about their realities. Such a reflection group was formed and is the main focus of this book, about which more details are provided in the chapters that follow.

# Chapter 2

# "Forget All You Learned at ____": The Role of Teacher Education

## Preamble

An ESL teacher called Mary has been in the classroom for many years and has seen and heard first-hand what teachers think and do (although most of this probably occurs at the subconscious level of thought) in order to be effective in a real classroom. Mary is a pseudonym, of course, but nevertheless represents a real teacher in the sense that I have known and heard much the same as you are about to hear, from many different "Marys" in many different parts of the world. Mary has witnessed a large number of novice teachers over her years and as she is a keen human observer she has watched as they have attempted to implement the knowledge they have obtained in their teacher education courses in their lessons with real students. She has also noted how they have struggled to match this theoretical knowledge with real students who are not responding. Indeed, Mary knows well after years of observing and even trying to help some novice teachers adjust to their new world that such theoretical knowledge could not be further from the truth, their *current teaching truth*, because its implementation does not work in practice. Mary rolls her eyes at what the novice teachers say they have learned in their teacher education courses about second language acquisition, phonetics, grammar and many more new methods that she has seen crop up over the years, because she thinks they are not much use in her classroom. Mary does not have anything against the content of these courses in their own right, and many of them seem interesting from the point of view of knowledge. But from the perspective of actual teaching practice, Mary feels that novice teachers are not properly prepared for the reality. In fact, Mary has no time for teacher educators and thinks that most of them are really out of touch with today's ESL classrooms. Thus when Mary is asked to help a novice teacher she quickly and readily gives the following advice: "Forget all you learned at _____" [fill in the name of the teacher education institution] because it will not work." Unfortunately, this is the advice novice teachers receive in many different schools throughout the world today from experienced teachers who have given up on teacher education programs. I myself have heard such teachers dispense this advice on three different continents.

### Reflective Break

- Has any teacher/mentor/supervisor/administrator told you "Forget all you learned at ____"?
- If yes, how did you react?
- If not, how would you react if someone said this to you?

## Introduction

The path to becoming an ESL teacher is as varied as the schools and methods of instruction a teacher can choose from. Most ESL teachers are trained in some formal manner—be it a weekend course, or a certificate, diploma or graduate degree program. As noted in the opening chapter many teacher educators, novice teachers, administrators and others assume that the knowledge that teachers are given in these training courses is relevant and useful to help them teach. Thus we say that this knowledge from teacher education programs and courses is transferable to the first year of teaching. However, the information and advice provided by "Mary" in the preamble would suggest otherwise.

This chapter will first revisit the notion of the transfer of knowledge gained in a teacher education course to the first year of teaching. Then it will lay out why it is important to discover exactly what novice teachers experience in their first year, and describe how the group of three novice teachers was set up and researched to record what the three of them experienced as they navigated their first semester as novice ESL teachers and how their teacher reflection group interacted throughout their various meetings. This chapter thus sets the scene for all the other chapters that will follow.

## Teacher Education: Whose Needs?

It seems that the TESOL profession is in a bit of a quandary: on the one hand we have language teacher educators providing the knowledge *they* consider important and necessary for trainees to become effective teachers; but on the other, we have some experienced language teachers (e.g., Mary above) who believe language teacher education programs are not providing the knowledge necessary for novice teachers to be effective in real classroom situations. Although the TESOL profession has been very slow to take up the discussion of the relevance of the content of teacher education programs to the reality of the classrooms their novice teachers will have to face, recently some TESOL educators have been voicing concerns about how qualified teachers really are (Faez & Vaelo, 2012; Farrell, 2015b).

For example, Farrell (2015b) has suggested that within TESOL, some teacher educators may have lost sight of whose needs these programs are actually addressing when preparing second language teachers: their own needs as academics or their novice teachers' needs? In agreement, Faez & Vaelo (2012) maintain that that teacher preparation programs should be reconsidered in order to work out how the program content could be aligned more closely with the needs of novice teachers. However, in order to be able to realign a language teacher education program to the needs of novice teachers, language teacher educators need to be aware of what those needs are. Although most teacher educators are probably aware that novice teachers face many issues and challenges in their first years, it is interesting to note that many TESOL programs still have limited information about how their graduates are faring in their induction years, or even what their work lives involve (Baecher, 2012). This is because not many studies exist about what novice ESL teachers actually experience in their first year, regardless of the context. Although recently there have been some attempts at examining the experiences of novice teachers in their first year, most of these have utilized mass surveys or questionnaires that can have some use but are limited to what the novice teachers want to report.

No in-depth case study of novice ESL teachers' experiences in their first year of teaching has been conducted that involves the use of reflective practice. Indeed, Wright (2010: 289) has noted the paucity of research within TESOL (and SLTE, or second language teacher education, in particular), further suggesting that we are falling behind research developments in general education. He has therefore called for more in-depth studies of "the encounters" experienced by participants in SLTE programs "so as to reach a greater understanding of how teachers learn."

## Reflective Break

- Why do you think there are not many accounts of the experiences of novice ESL teachers in the literature on teacher education?
- Do you think it would be easy or difficult to get these accounts? Explain your answer.

- Do you agree or disagree that some teacher educators may have lost sight of whose needs their courses and programs are actually addressing? Give reasons for your answer.
- When you answer the previous question think about specific examples from your teacher education course and say whose needs the course best addressed.

## Getting Their Story

Considering then that most literature reviews indicate insufficient case-study research on the real experiences of novice ESL teachers, the case study outlined and described in this book explores the experiences of three novice ESL teachers in Canada with the following as its main objectives:

- To investigate the practices that three novice ESL teachers consider, emphasize and integrate as they go about their work both inside and outside the classroom in their first semester of teaching.
- To examine the effect of various strategies and activities that can best foster critical reflection for novice ESL teachers so that we can initiate development of new principles and practices in second language teacher education programs (see chapter 9) and in the first year of teaching (see chapter 10).

From the documenting of these three novice ESL teachers' experiences I hope readers will gain a better understanding of their own teaching worlds. According to Bullough (1997: 19), telling such a story is "a way of getting a handle on what [they] believe, on models, metaphors and images that underpin action and enable meaning making, on [their] theories." In English language teaching, Freeman (1994) has pointed out the importance of listening to teachers' voices about what they do because he says that it is necessary to put teachers at the center of telling their stories. He maintains (ibid.: 89) that "putting teachers front and center in terms of listening to what they do follows the jazz maxim: 'You have to know the story in order to tell the story.'" In telling their story then, by relaying what they discussed in their group and with me, I hope you will see, as Bullough (1997: 19) noted, that through story-telling "personal beliefs become explicit." I will now outline the approach that was adopted to make their story explicit.

**Reflective Break**

- Why is it important to get the story of real novice teachers in their first year?
- How can we best get their story?

## Theoretical Approach

The theoretical framework employed in the study is grounded in the existing literature on teacher education and development from the field of TESOL, and comes under an overall framework that I refer to as "reflective language teaching." This framework views language teaching from three main perspectives (there are more of course): *teaching as reflection, teaching as a cognitive process* and *teaching as personal construction*. I will explain each one briefly as follows:

- *Teaching as reflection* is based on the assumption that teachers can learn from their *professional* experience through focused reflection on the nature and meaning of their teaching practices (Farrell, 2007, 2015a; Richards & Lockhart 1994; Wallace 1998). Reflection is viewed as the process of examination of these practices and this can lead to a better understanding of such practices. Reflection of this kind can include self-monitoring, journal-writing, classroom observation and engaging in group discussions (Farrell, 2004a, b, 2007, 2012b, 2015a; Richards & Farrell, 2005).
- *Teaching as a cognitive process* recognizes the complexity of the teaching act and examines the nature of novice teachers' beliefs, values and assumptions and how these influence the teaching act (Farrell & Lim, 2005; Woods, 1996). As Borg (2003: 81) suggests, "Teachers are active, thinking decision-makers who make instructional choices by drawing on complex practically-oriented, personalized, and context-sensitive networks of knowledge, thoughts, and beliefs."
- *Teaching as personal construction* is based on the belief that teacher knowledge is actively constructed by the teacher and learning is seen as involving reorganization and reconstruction of this knowledge, and it is through these processes that knowledge is internalized (Roberts 1998). In a teacher's professional development the emphasis is on the teacher's individual and personal contribution to the understanding of his/her practices, focusing on activities that foster the development of self-awareness and personal interpretation such as journal-writing and self-monitoring (Richards & Farrell, 2005, 2011).

## Methodology

Building on the theoretical framework described above, the research examined the reflections of three novice ESL college teachers. The study utilized qualitative methods of research that include a case-study approach (Merriam, 1988; Richards, 2003) that was exploratory and descriptive in nature (Bogdan & Bilken, 1982). The research also adopted an interpretivist perspective (Goetz & LeCompte, 1984). The case-study methodology was chosen because it best facilitates the construction of detailed, in-depth understanding of what is to be studied, and therefore can engage with complexity (Stake, 1995). Other TESOL scholars have successfully utilized such a case-study approach for similar types of research (e.g., Clair, 1998; Tsui, 2003). Clair (1998), for example, used this approach to report on a one-year study of the explorations of ESL teacher study groups in the USA when they came together to examine their teaching. Tsui (2003) also used a case-study approach to highlight how different forms of language teacher knowledge developed over time and contributed to development of teacher expertise. In addition, such case-study research can facilitate conceptual/theoretical development because existing theories can be brought up against complex realities, and the very richness of the data can help generate new thinking and fresh ideas about second language novice teacher education and development.

## Participants

The teacher group consisted of three female native English-speaking novice ESL teachers (each had just started their first year teaching ESL) who volunteered to come together for one semester (12 weeks) to reflect on their work together with a facilitator (the author). Each teacher had an initial qualification in teaching ESL (a BA in Applied Linguistics and a Certificate in Teaching English as a Second Language [TESL]), one had an MA in Applied Linguistics and the other two had certificates in TESL that qualified them to teach. All three were employed part-time in the same institution as ESL teachers. This institution ran an ESL program for international students at all proficiency levels of English as a second language. Most of these students intended to enroll in full-time courses in the same institution after they had successfully completed their English language courses; indeed, many of them had been granted conditional acceptance for such courses on condition that they passed an ESL course. The ESL teachers in that institution were aware that their students had to first pass their English language courses before being admitted to regular courses at the college.

As group facilitator, I managed the process as a whole so that the teacher-participants could have space in which to reflect on their own practice. In order to protect the identity of the teachers I have not given them any titles or pseudonyms but rather report the role identities that emerged from the group discussions as a whole. The teachers are "named" T1, T2 and T3 and I do not point out their characteristics for the same reasons of anonymity. I fully recognize that not giving a full description of each teacher leads to a severe limitation of the report (see chapter 10 for other limitations) but I do so for ethical reasons as they are only beginning their careers. I assure readers that the findings reported in each chapter are very real and instructional for many other novice teachers about to embark on their teaching careers. I present these findings in the hope that they will be of help in changing the situation so that the TESOL profession will stop eating its young (see chapter 1).

### Reflective Break

- Why is it important to protect the anonymity of the three ESL teachers in this book?
- Because I chose to protect the anonymity of the three novice ESL teachers I had to mix their descriptions and not give each of them a name, referring to them instead as T1, T2, T3. What issues does this raise for the report in the book?
- I only gave a brief outline of the teachers' education and qualifications, again to protect their identity. What problems might this cause?

## Data Collection and Analysis

Data was collected over a one-semester period (12 weeks) that constituted the winter term of a school year. All discussions were recorded and transcribed. All three novice teachers agreed to commit themselves as much as possible to the following: attend all group meetings, engage in classroom observations, write teaching journals and attend interviews.

- *Interviews*: An initial interview was conducted to elicit information about each teacher's life story at the beginning of the process. These interviews gave this author necessary background details pertaining to the ESL teachers' initial education experiences. Other interviews conducted after this consisted of questions on topics that came up during the course of the reflections in general or in the teaching journals, group discussions and/or classroom observations. All interviews were audio-recorded and transcribed.

- *Teaching journals*: The use of teaching journals in this study was as a means for the teachers to record their thoughts and reflections about their practice (Farrell, 2012b). Writing in teaching journals can assist novice teachers to focus on specific aspects of their development in their first year so that they can obtain new insights into their work (Richards & Farrell, 2005; Farrell, 2012b). In this study each participant agreed to write at least one entry after a professional "event" was experienced; an event included a class observation and/or discussion, and a group meeting.

- *Group discussions*: The group had weekly discussions (twelve in all) in which mutual understandings were constructed through talk (Mann, 2005). The group discussions followed Beaumont & O'Brien's (2000) suggestion of moving from chat to focused discussions that are specific to the participants' work. All group discussions were audio-recorded, transcribed and later coded for content.

- *Classroom observations*: Classroom observations were used to document the novice teachers' theories-in-use and the results were compared with their stated beliefs elicited during interviews and group discussions (Farrell, 2007). Each classroom observation was audio- and video-recorded to help facilitate recall of classroom events, because recall of these moments can provide insight into the relationship between the teachers' knowledge bases, reflective practices and classroom practices.

As group facilitator I attempted, as Osterman & Kottkamp (2004: 95) have proposed, to "create an environment that supports cooperative learning." Thus, throughout the reflection process I attempted to keep anxiety levels as low as possible by building an atmosphere of openness and trust. I shared my perceptions openly with the group as a participant-observer in the group discussions where appropriate (Clair, 1998); however, I did not reflect on my own teaching. Rather, I managed the process so that the teacher-participants could feel they had space in which to reflect on their own practice.

Data were analyzed on an ongoing and recursive basis (Glesne & Peshkin, 1992; Lincoln & Guba, 1985). During data analysis, the group discussions, classroom observations, interviews and teaching journals were coded using inductive analysis procedures (Johnson, 1992). Data analysis also incorporated some supplementary quantitative methods (Glesne & Peshkin, 1992) for tabulating the number of occurrences of specific topics when determining the teachers' knowledge.

In order to establish the trustworthiness (a qualitative measurement alternative to reliability and validity) of my findings, I (along with graduate research assistants who were trained in the coding techniques) assessed the quality of the data by checking for their "credibility" (Lincoln & Guba, 1985: 300). Lincoln & Guba suggest that "credible findings will be produced" by "the investment of sufficient time to achieve certain purposes: learning the culture, testing for misinformation introduced by distortions either of the self or the respondents, and building trust" (ibid.: 301). During data triangulation, a piece of evidence was compared and cross-checked with other kinds of evidence.

## Overall Guiding Framework

I decided to introduce an overall framework to guide the initial stage of the novice teacher reflection group meetings and journal writing. This framework arose out of my previous work with teacher groups and is grounded in the experiences of these groups (Farrell, 2007, 2014). However, I did not use it as a prescription but rather as a guide to help us get started, while at the same time remaining open to what the teachers wanted to continue or change, or to new items they might invent as we went along during the period of reflection. As it turned out, we followed most of the framework outlined below. The framework had four core elements: create opportunities for reflection, negotiate ground rules, make provisions for time and build trust. These core elements were not isolated but all connected as one built on the other and all needed to be considered as a whole (see Farrell, 2007). I now briefly outline the four components of this framework.

### *Create Opportunities for Reflection*

The first, and most important, component of the framework involves providing opportunities for language teachers to reflect through a range of approaches. These include exploring one's beliefs and classroom practices, classroom communication patterns and interaction, critical incidents, language proficiency and use of metaphors and maxims (see also Farrell, 2015a). These were explored by such reflective tools as group discussions, journal writing and classroom observations. The teachers had the opportunity to use any of these reflective tools alone or combination with each other. The group meetings created the most opportunities for sustained concentration and discussion in which understandings of practice were constructed through talk. These discussions were recorded, transcribed and later analyzed for what issues occurred most frequently, as noted above. The journals were also analyzed. Providing these opportunities for novice teachers to reflect was only the first component of this model of reflection. In order to establish an atmosphere where reflective practice is encouraged, several conditions must be met. These conditions include the other elements of the framework: negotiating ground rules, providing for different types of time, and providing for a low affective state.

## Negotiate Ground Rules

The framework called for the group to negotiate a set of built-in rules or guidelines that the group and each novice teacher would agree to follow in order to focus their reflections over a period of time. For example, if teachers have decided to reflect in a group, they must consider who will chair the group meetings. One answer might be to have a different chairperson for each meeting with various levels of responsibility (e.g. to provide a venue and refreshments, and set the agenda and length of the meetings). As it turned out, as group facilitator I chaired all of the meetings as the novice teachers agreed that this was the most comfortable way to conduct the discussions. Of course, all of the above activities and built-in guidelines cannot be accomplished quickly; like all valuable things, they take time. This introduces the next important component of the model: time.

## Make Time

For teachers to be able to reflect on their work, time is a very important consideration and a vital commodity. For novice teachers this is especially challenging because of the newness of their context, and all that goes into beginning to teach. Again, using the model of reflection, I suggested that the teachers consider three different kinds of time and that they should define each type themselves before entering into the reflective process. These three are: individual time, activity time and period of reflection time.

- *Individual time*: Practicing teachers (both novice and experienced) are kept very busy in their daily teaching and other related duties, and the amount of time any one teacher is willing to invest in his or her professional self-development will naturally vary. As I mentioned above, for novice teachers this is especially true because everything they do is practically new for them. This can create a dilemma for the group if all the participants do not attend all the group meetings or participate fully in the activities; group cohesion may be harmed. Therefore, a certain level of commitment by individual participants in terms of time availability should be negotiated by the group at the start of the process. All three novice teachers, although they were very busy, agreed to one semester of intense reflections (weekly group meetings) and also consented to be interviewed about their experiences.

- *Activity time*: Associated with the time each participant has to give to reflection is the time needed for specific activities related to the compiling of material for reflection. For example, for classroom observations, the number of times a class is to be observed should be negotiated ahead while also taking the first notion of time (individual) into consideration. The journal also needs time: time to write and time to read. Our group meetings turned out to be about one hour each in duration; each teacher undertook to write their journals as often as they could; and although they agreed to frequent classroom observations, these did not occur with much frequency throughout the period of reflection.
- *Period of reflection time*: The final aspect of time concerns the reflective period as a whole that teachers are willing to commit to. Teachers should keep two important points in mind when considering how long they want to reflect. One, they should remember that critical reflection on one's teaching takes time, so the reflective period should be comparatively long rather than short; otherwise, it might be time wasted. In addition, when teachers commit to having a fixed period in which to reflect, they need to identify an exact time slot that they can devote wholly to reflection.

## Build Trust

The components of the framework on reflective language teaching outlined above all pose some threat and associated anxiety for novice teachers when they engage in reflective teaching for any period of time. Therefore, a non-threatening environment should be encouraged by building up trust, especially where peers and/or groups are observing each other and are involved in group discussions. Ways of establishing trust can be incorporated into the reflective process itself, such as emphasizing description and observation over judgment in classroom observations and group discussions. Although all three novice teachers worked together, they did not know each other well before the group was formed. So we started slowly, giving ourselves time to build up trust in the process and in each other. For example, the first meeting was just talking about creating opportunities for reflection as well as making the different provisions for time, as outlined above. After this first meeting the group discussion format generally followed a method of moving from chat (usually initiated by this author as facilitator in the first five meetings) to more focused discussions that were specific to the participants' work issues. What follows in this chapter is an outline and discussion of the overall communications and interpersonal climate of the group, before going into more detailed analysis of specific issues and topics that were discussed during the group meetings.

> **Reflective Break**
>
> - Examine each aspect of the overall guiding framework and discuss how you would negotiate each if you were a member of a novice teacher reflection group. (You will revisit the idea of novice teacher reflection groups again in chapter 10.)
> - Which of these would be easy to negotiate and which would be difficult, and why?

## Setting the Scene

As mentioned before, this group of three novice teachers agreed to meet each week for 12 weeks (the first meeting was for orientation purposes) for one-hour group meetings. As we considered this a group of teachers reflecting together, rather than three individual teachers, I now present some overall communication findings in terms of the group as a whole. As McDermott & Roth (1978: 321) have pointed out, "A person's behavior is best described in terms of the behavior of those immediately about the person." I present the details of the conversations in subsequent chapters, but here I will set the scene for the group by giving an overall picture of the communication and interpersonal climate during the group discussions.

## Interpersonal Group Climate and Communication

Whenever a group of people get together for regular discussions it is inevitable that the group develops a "personality" type of its own independent of the individuals that comprise it. I do not want to state, however, that the individual voices within the group do not have their own unique personality as well (each person should and does have an individual identity); rather the individuals together form the group that in turn develops its own identity. When the three novice ESL teachers met with the facilitator to reflect on their first-year experiences, this group also developed its own identity in which participants communicated with each other for the common goal of reflecting on practice. Within such communications the group developed its own interpersonal climate in which participants attended meetings, made statements, asked and answered questions. These communications continued throughout the life of the group. So, in order to lay the foundations for analysis of the details of the group discussions, I first want give readers an overall view of the discussions so that they can see what patterns of communication developed during the whole process. I then present a snapshot of individual group discussions to show the communication flows (through sociograms) so that readers can also get a feel of what transpired in these meetings. This graphic representation of the group discussions will give readers a better understanding of how the participants interacted and what patterns of communications developed during these interactions, as the group moved from the second meeting (I did not analyze the first meeting as it was an orientation meeting with the facilitator doing most of the talking) to the eleventh one (I also did not analyze the twelfth meeting as it was the last one).

I first present the overall interpersonal climate of these ten group discussions by attempting to answer the following questions:

- Who received more communication?
- Who was absent?
- Who asked the most questions to individuals or the group? (potential leader)
- Which pairs communicated most?

Table 2.1 presents the answers to the questions posed above.

From a global perspective, two different patterns of interaction seem to have emerged in the group. For example, meetings two to five show that the group facilitator was more active than the other participants, while meetings six to eleven show a slightly different pattern of interaction with the other teachers receiving more communications. In the earlier meetings, the group facilitator initiated and received most of the communication. This is probably because the teachers were still getting to know one another. On the other hand, the later meetings showed a slightly different pattern of communication with the T1, T2 and T3 beginning to take more control over who they communicated directly with. Table 2.2 gives more of a detailed indication of this change when looking at the frequencies of the total number of utterances directed at each participant for each meeting.

Table 2.1: Interpersonal Group Climate

| Questions | Group Meetings | | | | | | | | | |
|---|---|---|---|---|---|---|---|---|---|---|
| | 2 | 3 | 4 | 5 | 6 | 7 | 8 | 9 | 10 | 11 |
| Who received more communication? | T | T | T | T | T<br>T2 | T<br>T1 | T<br>T2 | T<br>T2 | T<br>T3 | T<br>T1 |
| Who was absent? | – | – | – | – | – | T2 | – | – | T1 | T2 |
| Who asked the most questions? | T | T | T | T | T<br>T2 | T | T | T2 | T | T<br>T1<br>T3 |
| Who spoke to whom? | T+T1<br>T+T2<br>T+T3 | T+T2<br>T+T3 | T+T2 | T+T1<br>T+T2 | T+T2<br>T+T3<br>T1+T2<br>T1+T3<br>T2+T3 | T+T1<br>T1+T3<br>T2+T3 | T+T2<br>T1+T2<br>T2+T3 | T+T1<br>T+T2<br>T1+T2<br>T2+T3 | T+T2<br>T+T3 | T+T1<br>T+T3 |

Note: T indicates the facilitator; T+T2 indicates the facilitator and teacher 2.

**Table 2.2:** Total Utterances Directed at Each Participant

| Group Meetings | Direct Communication Received | | | | | | | | | |
|---|---|---|---|---|---|---|---|---|---|---|
| | **2** | **3** | **4** | **5** | **6** | **7** | **8** | **9** | **10** | **11** |
| T | 122 | 174 | 108 | 165 | 95 | 105 | 148 | 151 | 134 | 119 |
| T1 | 46 | 110 | 61 | 103 | 66 | 192 | 88 | 151 | – | 124 |
| T2 | 56 | 99 | 74 | 100 | 101 | – | 124 | 206 | 94 | – |
| T3 | 55 | 95 | 47 | 47 | 95 | 162 | 165 | 122 | 118 | 76 |

As can be observed in table 2.2, from group meeting number six onwards (except for meeting ten), the group facilitator (T), received less communications than at least one of the other novice teachers. Thus, meetings two to five may be called phase I of the group process, while phase II includes the remainder of the meetings (meetings six to eleven).

In order to look at the patterns of interaction in more detail, each of the meetings was analyzed schematically by constructing a group interaction sociogram (Moreno, 1953). The communication patterns of the group participants in each meeting after the first one were charted in these sociograms. A group sociogram is constructed by:

1. Drawing a square for each member indicating seating arrangements.
2. Drawing an arrow for each speaker's speech, with the total number of comments/questions written beside the line and the arrow pointing in the direction of the comment.
3. Drawing an arrow that points outward when a participant's comment was directed at the group rather than toward a specific individual, with the number of such comments indicated beside the line.

Figure 2.1 is an example of a typical early group sociogram and figure 2.2 shows a typical later group sociogram (because of space restrictions not all the sociograms can be reproduced here).

Figure 2.1 gives a visual of the interaction of the participants during meeting two. It shows that T, the group facilitator, was the most active—as is to be expected in the initial group meetings. For example, this sociogram shows that the facilitator directed a lot of questions to the group (51) and also asked and answered many questions in interaction with individual group members, whose interactions with each other were much less frequent. In contrast, figure 2.2 gives a different picture from a later meeting, meeting eight, where T, the facilitator, asks less questions and the three novice teachers participate much more. This indicates that the teachers

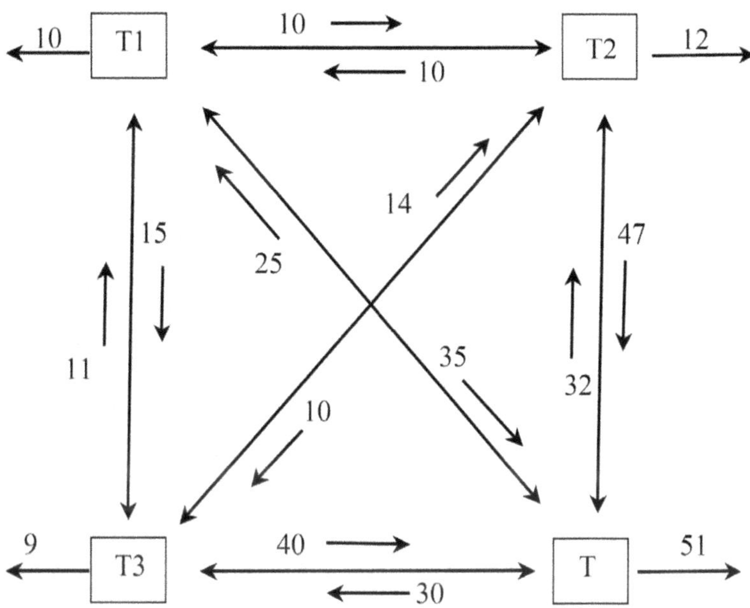

Figure 2.1: Group Sociogram for Meeting Two

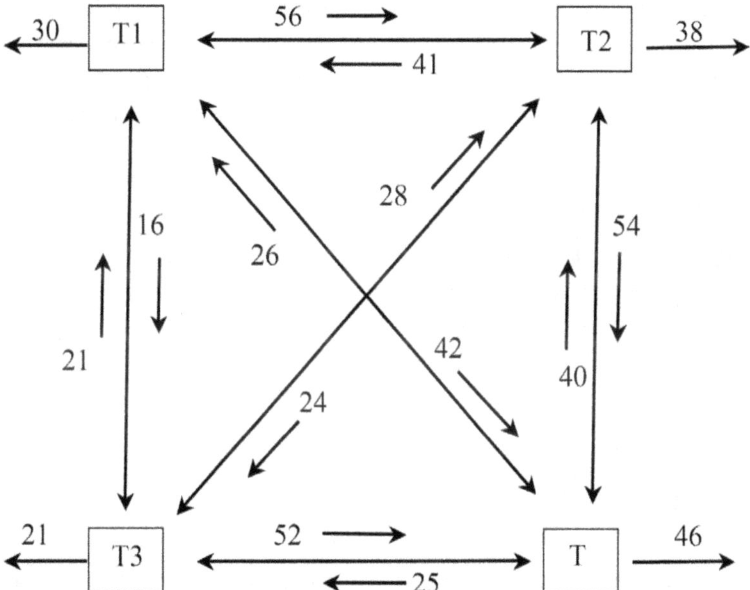

Figure 2.2: Group Sociogram for Meeting Eight

now felt more comfortable posing questions to the group and each other than they did in the first five meetings.

The tables and figures above highlight the changing patterns of interaction during the different phases of the group meetings. For example, the first phase recognized above could be seen as a developmental phase where the facilitator takes more responsibility to provide opportunities for reflection by encouraging the participants to talk and interact with each other. In this first phase it is probably natural for participants to be tentative in their contributions. Trust takes time to develop and this group is no exception as it seems the participants only got comfortable interacting with each other from the sixth group meeting onwards (see figure 2.2 for the sociogram of meeting eight). Although none of the three novice teachers emerged as an outright leader in the discussions from meeting number six onwards, all three did take on more responsibility for keeping discussions going by posing lots of questions to each other. That said, the sociograms above present some idea of the complexity of interactions in such groups. Future groups of teachers wanting to reflect on their work will have to confront and define these issues if they want to obtain the maximum benefits from such meetings. What the sociograms do not show, however, was the huge level of support each participant received from the group as a whole. This level of support is demonstrated in the chapters that follow when details of the eleven group discussions are outlined and analysed. The chapters that follow are not necessarily in the order of the frequency of discussion of their topics (although I point out the frequency count of the topic/issue in each chapter); rather they are ordered in terms of when the discussions of these topics occurred (chronological order) in the semester.

## Reflective Break

- What is your initial impression of the interpersonal climate of the group from tables 1.1 and 1.2 above?
- What important information do the sociograms in figures 1.1 and 1.2 provide about how individual meetings progressed from a general point of view?

## Conclusion

This chapter suggests that teacher educators must reconsider whose needs are being met when novice ESL teachers go through their programs: their own needs or those of the novice teachers? This is not at all clear, as many novice teachers continue to suffer through their first year on the job with the perception that they have not been adequately prepared for real classrooms. What is also shocking is that there are not many accounts of the experiences of novice ESL teachers in their first year of teaching. However, this knowledge is essential for teacher educators and novice teachers alike, if the latter are to successfully navigate their complex first year as teachers. Thus the chapter has made a case for this study of the story and experiences of three novice ESL teachers during their first semester (12 weeks) of teaching in Canada. The chapter has outlined the method of data gathering and analysis, as well as the overall framework that guided the research presented in this book. The interpersonal climate of the group meetings has been summarized here, to give the overall picture before going into details of the particular topics they talked about, that are the subject of subsequent chapters.

# Chapter 3

# From Trainee to Teacher: The Transition Shock

## Introduction

When pre-service teachers (sometimes called trainee teachers or learner teachers) enter a teacher education program they do so in order to acquire the skills they will need to carry out their profession of teaching, be it the teaching of a content subject like science or of English as a second language. When they graduate from these programs they are considered "qualified" by many (especially by administrators) because they have successfully completed the requirements of that program. As a result, most people (including the novice teachers themselves) think they have gained knowledge about various aspects of teaching and learning.

The "qualified" ESL teacher, now called a novice teacher, is deemed ready to begin his or her career in a real school and classroom with real students—in this particular context teaching English to speakers of other languages. Thus the teacher will begin his or her transition from trainee to novice teacher most likely with great anticipation of a smooth entry into the profession as a "qualified" ESL teacher. Some novice teachers do make such a smooth transition but unfortunately some do not, with damaging results for the novice teachers, their students, their colleagues, the school and the government agencies that may have funded their training—especially if these novice teachers decide to quit the profession. For many novice teachers, regardless of the subject they are teaching, the transition from the training program comes as somewhat of a shock because the reality of where they find themselves is very different to the comfort of the teacher education program where kind and caring educators catered to their almost every need.

This chapter describes this transition from trainee to novice teacher in real classrooms and specifically focuses on the "shock" many novice teachers experience as they attempt to navigate through the difficult first year. It begins by examining the transition from two perspectives: real classroom teaching as well as working with colleagues. This discussion then sets the scene for a discussion of the "shock" that many novice teachers feel, as well as the specific challenges they face during their first year of teaching. The findings of this chapter once again highlight the need to confront the reality of what novice teachers experience.

## Reflective Break

- Do you feel "qualified" and ready to teach?
- Do you think all or any of the knowledge that you obtained in your teacher education course can be transferred into your practice in a real classroom?
- If yes, why—what did you do in your credential program that prepares you to teach?
- If not, why not—what did you not do in your credential program that you feel is necessary to prepare you to teach?

## From Trainee to Novice Teacher

Most novice teachers arrive at their new school probably a bit nervous but excited and enthusiastic (they have been referred to as "spark-plug go-getters" [Kaufmann & Ring, 2011: 52]) about their future career. Most are eager to get into *their own classroom* because they have experienced teaching in classrooms during their teaching practice in which they were guests and supervised by their cooperating teacher who was most likely the regular teacher of that class. Indeed the students they were teaching during the practicum were probably different too because they also realized that the "new" teacher was practicing and as such "not to be taken seriously" (a real comment I heard some years ago). So the novice teachers are eager to get into the classroom and make it *their own* after they meet *their* students. In addition, when they were on teaching practice, they were introduced (hopefully) to some other teachers in that school placement but they probably felt that they were not viewed or treated as real colleagues, so now in their first days, they are eager to be viewed as equal colleagues, though most are also willing to learn from their more experienced colleagues. I will discuss each briefly in turn: teaching in the real classroom and interacting with colleagues.

> **Reflective Break**
>
> - If you are still in your teacher education program, how do you think you will feel as you walk into your new school on your first day as a novice teacher?
> - If you are a novice teacher, how did you feel the first day you walked into your new school?
> - What is your understanding of the term used to describe a novice teacher: "spark-plug go-getter"? Do you think it describes you? Do you have any other terms you would use to describe yourself as a novice teacher?
> - What issues do you expect to face in a real classroom?
> - How do you think you will relate to new colleagues?

## The Classroom

Although novice teachers may be confident about their ability to teach in a real classroom and many think that they can now actually begin teaching for the first time, they are in fact still continuing what was started in their teacher education program: *learning to teach*. Indeed, while most novices may draw a line under what they have experienced before and just "go in and teach," whatever they end up doing in their new classroom is still very much influenced (whether they are aware of this or not) by events that have occurred long before. These influences include their years of schooling as students themselves (elementary, middle, high school etc.) as well as the impact of the knowledge from the teacher education program they have just graduated from.

So when novice language teachers enter a real classroom to teach for the first time, they have already accumulated an array of (usually tacitly held) prior assumptions, beliefs and knowledge about teaching and learning. We may think then that because novice teachers have spent all this time (fifteen or sixteen years) in or around classrooms in their role as student, they would as a result find it easy to adapt to their new role as teacher in a their own classroom. This seems plausible because novice teachers think they know classrooms from their prior experiences: how classrooms work, how teachers move and talk and how students respond (or do not respond); in fact, many have probably played teacher games when they were younger. So the transformation from student to language teacher should not be too difficult; indeed I have heard many who do not teach say: "just go in and talk." However, as you will read later in this chapter, during this first year, a novice teacher's prior assumptions, beliefs and mainly positive attitudes that were built up during his or her student years and reconfirmed in many cases during the teacher education program and courses, can be "buffeted and challenged as they [truly] learn about teaching" (Loughran, Brown & Doecke, 2001: 9) in real classrooms with real students, and as they learn about interacting with real colleagues—the next aspect of learning in the first year.

## Reflective Break

- Do you agree that novice teachers are still influenced by events that have occurred long before they commence their first year?
- If yes, what are these influences?
- If not, why not?
- Do you agree that the transition from student to teacher is not simple? Why, or why not?
- How would a novice teacher's positive attitudes be "buffeted and challenged" during his or her first year?

## Colleagues

So, not only do novice teachers have to get to grips with the reality of adjusting to life in real classrooms during their first year, they also must adjust to life in a real school with colleagues who have been in that school for some time so are very familiar with its routines and happenings. When a novice teacher walks into a school of strangers, all of whom know each other and seem busy getting on with their worlds, this poses a particular challenge. The novice teacher must quickly adjust to working with this new group of people who have an already established, well-defined daily routine and may not have time (or so it seems) to stop to help the novice break into this routine and fit in with the new group.

The novice teacher thus finds himself or herself suddenly immersed in a new world that has an established professional culture with "particular goals and shared values and standards of conduct" (Calderhead, 1992: 6). This professional world though is not a place where its long-standing members any longer articulate or even question what they have already established, so how does the novice teacher figure out their goals, values and standards, or where these came from? The other teachers no longer articulate these as they all know them by now, which leaves the novice teacher in a bind because he or she must try adjust to this new professional culture and social world without being explicitly informed about it. How can the novice teacher for example learn the "established" rules so that he or she can interact with his or her new colleagues in a way that recognizes their relative positions? Of course, as anyone who has been accepted as a new member of a club knows, this process of social adjustment to this new professional culture and social world will take time. As Schutz (1989: 32) has noted, it is important for the novice teacher to understand that entry will be "a continuous process of inquiry into the cultural pattern of the approached group." Unfortunately, the group in which the novice teacher seeks to gain entry may not be as accommodating as it should, and may not want to recognize new members until enough of them think the new member has "earned his or her spurs." Thus making the transition from the teacher education to the classroom and the school is anything but a simple process and the novice teacher will inevitably suffer some "shocks" along the way, the severity of which will depend on how well the teacher was prepared (or not prepared) during the teacher education program, especially how (or if) they have been prepared to take risks during their first year (Reid, 2011).

## Reflective Break

- Why would novice teachers have to consider how they will interact with their new colleagues?
- How would a novice teacher break into the professional world/ culture of his or her new school?
- Why would novice teachers be considered strangers in a new school?
- What goals, values and standards would a novice teacher's new colleagues have already established?
- What is your understanding of the idea that the novice teacher undergoes "a continuous process of inquiry into the cultural pattern of the approached group"?

## The "Shock"

As mentioned above, the transition from the teacher education program to the first year of teaching is a complex one and different labels have been used in the research literature to characterize it. For example, the transition from learning to teach to teaching to learn has been called a "transition shock" (Corcoran, 1981), a "praxis shock" (Kelchtermans & Ballet, 2002), a "cultural shock (Wideen, Mayer-Smith

& Moon, 1998) and a "transfer shock" Cejda, 1997). The common term of course is the word "shock" and this is because, as has already been pointed out, some novice teachers from the moment they begin their teaching careers suddenly see a "collapse of the missionary ideals" formed during their teacher education course, replaced "by the harsh and rude reality of classroom life" (Veenman, 1984: 143).

This "shock" is not limited to the teaching profession; it happens in many other professions as well, such as medicine where doctors (Flynn & Hekelman, 1993) have reported difficult transitions into the real workplace, as well as engineering (Riordan & Goodman, 2007) and social work (O'Connor & Dalgleish, 1986). Indeed, not only is "shock" a common term in the literature to describe how novice teachers see the transition, but it also seems to be a worldwide phenomenon for novice teachers regardless of the subject matter they are teaching. Worldwide research on this transition in the educational field supports the idea that most novice teachers experience some kind of "shock" when transitioning into real classrooms in their first year of teaching; for example, from Europe: Belgium (Kelchtermans & Ballet, 2002), Africa: Botswana (Tafa, 2004), and Asia: Hong Kong (So & Watkins, 2005).

In all of these contexts, after their first experiences in real classrooms novice teachers have had the common "shock" of some kind of collapse of their ideals and expectations that were built up by during their teacher education programs, which may be called a "reality shock." Novice teachers who experience such a reality shock begin to wonder why they choose teaching as a career and this shock impacts their sense and feelings of belonging to the profession which in turn influences their capacity to teach effectively during this first year. As Rogers & Babinski (2002: 1) put it: "False expectations, shattered dreams, and serious attacks on one's competence and self-worth—these are the all too common experiences of beginning teachers." If the differences between their expectations and the reality of the first year are large (i.e. if they are adversely affected by the transfer) then novice teachers will struggle in the transition period, which in turn will lead to stress, that in turn adversely affects their teaching—leading to a negative outcome for their students, and possible teacher attrition.

Although I mentioned some numbers related to teacher attrition in chapter 1, I want to return and reveal some other startling numbers of teacher attrition in the United States (regardless of the subject matter of teaching) to show just how important this issue of the impact of transfer shock is, though it is not given any attention in the field of TESOL. Research has indicated that 24 per cent of *all* novice teachers in the U.S. leave teaching within the first two years of starting their job, 33 per cent drop out after three years of teaching and between 40 and 50 per cent leave the teaching profession within their first five years on the job

(Joiner & Edwards, 2008). Indeed, research has reported that approximately 50 to 70 per cent of people entering TESOL leave the profession within three to five years (Phillips, 1989). Although this research is dated, what is clear is that novice teachers are still leaving the profession and this comes at an enormous cost—both human and financial. Consequently, it is clear that the transition shock is something that should be tackled within every profession, but especially the teaching profession if we are to have any hope of putting an end to "eating our young" through teacher attrition.

This means that we as a profession must begin to ask some hard questions about what is happening to our novice teachers and how we can better understand their experiences. If we do that we can do more to intervene and stop the high levels of teacher attrition. One important question that must be asked first is: Are these shocks that novice teachers experience primarily the result of being badly prepared in teacher education programs (the result of a lack of practical preparation), or the consequence of a lack of support from the school in which they are teaching during their first year, or the fault of the novice teachers themselves? I will discuss this question in the next section.

## Reflective Break

- What kind of ideals about teaching English to speakers of other languages did you have when you entered your teacher education program?
- Do you think your ideals are realistic, or have been realistic if you are now a novice teacher in a real classroom?
- Why do you think some have said that teachers should be prepared for "the harsh reality of the classroom"? What can be "harsh"?
- Do you agree that some novice teachers have "missionary ideals" that may be unrealistic?
- Why do you think the transition from your teacher education program to a real classroom could be a shock?
- Did you get a shock? If yes, what kind of shock? If not, what prepared you for the real classroom?

## The Blame Game

If we look at teacher preparation first in terms of whom to blame for novice teachers experiencing transition shocks during their first year, there is no shortage of research reports. Some blame the teacher education programs, some the school in which they are teaching in their first year. Although I will separate each, I think you will note that it is probably a combination of the two not working, and of course novice teachers themselves must take some responsibility for building up their ability to cope along with becoming professionally involved in the new school and articulating their needs and attempting to interact as closely as possible with new colleagues. I address these subjects in detail in chapters 9 and 10 with suggestions based on the results of the experiences of the three novice ESL teachers during their first year, but for now I will outline what research has been conducted on who is to blame.

Some time ago in TESOL Freeman (1994) cautioned language educators and novice teachers alike that most of what is presented in language teacher education programs may be washed away by the first-year experiences of becoming a novice teacher, a point also confirmed later in research studies by Richards (1998) and by Farrell (2003). In addition, Tarone & Allwright (2005) have reported that language teacher education programs may be at fault because they are not delivering relevant content that novice language teachers can implement in real classroom settings; as they have argued: "differences between the academic course content in language teacher preparation programs and the real conditions that novice language teachers are faced with in the language classroom appear to set up a gap that cannot be bridged by beginning teacher learners" (ibid.: 12). Indeed, Dellar (1990: 63) identified a series of difficulties that novice teachers reported they faced, such as problems of control, insufficient training, inappropriate methodology and difficulties in lesson planning. In Dellar's opinion, the difficulties the novice teachers faced were due to "a discrepancy between the content of IT [initial training], and what was ultimately expected of teachers in the school" (ibid.: 63).

In terms of perceptions of how teachers have been prepared for their first year, a lot of studies conducted worldwide have suggested that many novice language teachers feel they have not been adequately prepared. For example, studies conducted in the following countries have reported that novice teachers perceived that they were not adequately prepared for reality of their first year: Australia (O'Neill & Stephenson, 2014), China (Lewis, Romi, Qui & Katz, 2005), the UK (Merrett & Wheldall, 1993) and the USA (Hammond Stoughton, 2007), to mention a few. Most of these studies reported that the novice teachers pointed out a disconnect between what they were provided with during their teacher education programs and the reality of what they were experiencing in the schools.

Research on who is to blame for the shocks novice teachers experience during their first year also points the finger at the schools in which they must teach. Most schools expect novice teachers to be fully responsible for their teaching (after all this is the reason they were hired as qualified teachers) yet these teachers do not have the experience to draw on as their more experienced colleagues have, should they need to make any sudden adjustments. Some schools have some kind of induction program for novice teachers to help them through these adjustments, with some even appointing mentors, but this is not uniform across all schools as reported in the research.

Indeed, research has also cautioned that the mere appointment of a mentor is no guarantee the novice teacher will be successfully socialized into the school (Farrell, 2003). Farrell's (2003) case study of the socialization and development of one English language teacher into the profession, for example, revealed that even though a mentor was officially appointed by the school to the novice teacher, the teacher never had any further contact with this mentor beyond the introduction on the first day.

In addition, studies have reported that several novice teachers may have had no induction programs and were simply left on their own to cope in a "sink-or-swim" type situation (Varah, Theune & Parker, 1986). For example, in the Netherlands, many novice teachers have reported "that they were left to their own resources" (Brouwer & Korthagen, 2005: 202) and in Botswana novice teachers reported that they were "thrown in at the deep end in a 'sink or swim' fashion with no formal programme of induction" (Tafa, 2004: 757).

Thus, the research suggests that blame for the shocks that novice teachers have reported is shared between teacher education programs and schools alike, with some overlap, in that the novice teachers may discover that they have been set up in their teacher education courses (and teaching practice) for teaching approaches that do not work in real classrooms or equally that the school culture prohibits implementation of these approaches (Farrell, 2012a; Shin, 2012). What is clear is that novice teachers are far from the finished product as they make the transition from learning to teach to teaching to learn, and as such have to work on several more dimensions of learning to teach before they can teach effectively. The challenge, however, is how to accomplish these two complex tasks at the same time—continuing to learn how to teach while teaching others to learn.

## Reflective Break

- Did you think you were left in a "sink or swim" type of situation in your novice year?
- How should teachers be prepared for the real classroom?
- Do you think you were prepared well in your teacher education program for real classrooms?

- Examine in detail the problems below reported in Dellar (1990) by teachers who felt they had been inadequately trained for real classrooms. Explain your experiences with each and how you think novice teachers could be better prepared to tackle them:
  o Taking control in the classroom;
  o Insufficient training: dealing with monolingual classes, and issues related to students' use of their first language;
  o Inappropriate methodology: over-emphasis on oral skills at the expense of reading and writing, and inappropriate use of pair-work and group-work;
  o Lesson planning difficulties: bad timing, lack of variety, and spending too much time in preparation.
- What kind of support do novice teachers need in their first year?
- Did you get any support during your first year as a novice teacher? If yes, explain the nature of the support. If not, why not?
- What kind of induction program would best suit a novice teacher?
- Are mentors useful and what roles should a mentor play?

## From Learning to Teach, to Teaching to Learn

As stated above, novice teachers have the complex task of moving from learning to teach to teaching effectively or teaching to learn. This is because novice teachers are *still* learning and developing while they are teaching. Thus they are still working on developing several aspects of their practice in their first year (many of which were introduced during their teaching practice). Some of these dimensions include (among others) developing their *discourse skills*, their *teaching skills* and their overall *professional knowledge* (see Richards & Farrell, 2011 for a complete list).

### Discourse Skills

Novice teachers may have learned jargon associated with teaching during their teacher education program, such as "learner-centeredness," "learner autonomy," "task-based instruction" and so on, that help identify them as language teachers and help them interact with other teachers in their new setting. However, Richards & Farrell (2011) suggest that novice teachers must continue to acquire classroom discourse skills that can only really be developed while they are teaching in real classrooms. For example they must be able to provide language input at an appropriate level (comprehensible input) for their learners by using appropriate speech that is comprehensible (Richards & Farrell, 2011, call this "teacher talk") while at the same time providing specific opportunities for interactive and collaborative uses of language among learners. The development of such classroom discourse skills takes time and experience, and novice teachers will need to be aware of how their learners are reacting (or not reacting) to all of what they say while they teach.

## Teaching Skills

In their first year, novice teachers will probably try many different teaching approaches and methods that they learned in a sheltered environment (e.g., micro-teaching or teaching practice). However, they must be careful not to become frustrated if these methods do not seem to work immediately and should not resort to teaching the same way as they were taught when they were students because it seemed "to work." Novice teachers must have the confidence to try to develop a repertoire of varied routines and procedures suited to different kinds of learners so that they can become flexible in their teaching. They must be willing to take risks to depart from what their teachers did, or from the established routines and procedures of their new school, so that they can improvise and generate their own solutions to whatever challenges they are faced with. As Senior (2006: 157) notes, teachers must be able to sidestep by "bringing in little extra bits and pieces" as they develop their repertoire of teaching skills.

As they develop their teaching skills, novice teachers will also continue to develop their "pedagogical reasoning skills" as they gain experience in analyzing lesson content, begin to anticipate and resolve problems that occur during the lesson as well as develop their ability to make appropriate instructional decisions. In order to further develop these pedagogical reasoning skills it will be important for novice teachers to be able to reflect on their teaching *while* they teach (reflection-in-action), *after* they teach (reflection-on-action) and *before* they teach (reflection-for-action) (Farrell, 2015a).

## Professional Knowledge

During their teacher education program, pre-service teachers probably learned various foundational theories and practices that covered different kinds of knowledge such as disciplinary knowledge (knowledge related to language, linguistics, pedagogy) and pedagogical content knowledge (knowledge related to teaching such as curriculum planning, teaching the skill areas, assessment). During these courses it is assumed that the disciplinary knowledge, although it is not intended to have practical applications to the classroom, is important for teachers to have when they begin teaching; and that pedagogical content knowledge can help deliver the content from the disciplinary knowledge to their students. However, the successful implementation of this professional knowledge (disciplinary and pedagogical) is not guaranteed in a real classroom during the first year of teaching because not all teacher education programs emphasize every aspect of this professional knowledge for teachers in training. In fact there is great discrepancy in what different teacher education programs provide around the world, with many just promoting disciplinary knowledge over pedagogical content knowledge and thus making the transition for novice teachers more challenging. As Richards & Farrell (2011: 28) maintain, "we would expect novice teachers with a sound grounding in relevant pedagogical content knowledge to be better prepared than teachers without such knowledge to understand learners' needs, to diagnose learners' learning problems, to plan suitable instructional goals for lessons, and to select and design learning tasks."

During their teacher education program, novice teachers have probably experienced different contexts for their practice teaching, such as private schools or public institutions with mixed-level learners, or institutions offering courses in EAP (English for academic purposes), ESP (English for specific purposes) or ESL (Richards & Farrell, 2011). As they attempt to apply the knowledge they learned in their teacher education programs, they probably realize that each context has something different to offer and presents different challenges to overcome, including discovering what the "hidden curriculum" is in order to be able to function in a particular school context. Now that they have entered a new school context, novice teachers will need to acquire the appropriate contextual information (e.g., the nature of the school culture and its expectations, the existing knowledge levels of the students and their linguistic backgrounds) in order to be able to function effectively in that school context. Thus, learning to teach in the first year entails that novice teachers understand the specific values, norms of practice and patterns of social participation of their new school context so that they can integrate as smoothly as possible.

### Reflective Break

- How can novice teachers develop their classroom discourse skills to support classroom language learning?
- How can novice teachers develop their identity during their first year? Which has the most influence on identity development, the attitude of the novice teacher or the school context?

- What particular teaching skills do novice teachers need to develop during their first year?
- How can novice teachers apply both disciplinary knowledge and pedagogical content knowledge during their first year? Which is more important?
- Why do you think it is important for novice teachers to start to theorize from practice and thus become generators of knowledge rather than consumers of knowledge during their first year?

## Confronting the "Shock"

How then can we as a profession help novice teachers to get over the shock and adapt successfully to their new world? The above overview of the issues and challenges that novice teachers face in their first year suggests that it is important for language teacher educators to be able to identify and address these various influences and challenges so that their students will be able to adapt successfully into their new professional world. The TESOL profession cannot wait in the hope that a novice teacher's enthusiasm or vocational call to teach will get him or her through the first year successfully after graduating from a teacher education program. As a profession we need to better prepare novice teachers to have as smooth as possible a transition from their teacher education program to their first year of teaching. In order to be able to do this we must know in detail of what exactly novice teachers experience during their first year, not what we think they will experience as is the case in many teacher education programs today (Farrell, 2015b). In a wake-up call for the TESOL profession Mattheoudakis stated, relatively recently: "the truth is that we know very little about what actually happens" to novice teachers once they graduate from teacher education institutions and enter real classrooms (2007: 1273).

In fact, Mattheoudakis is correct and we as a profession need to understand in detail the "shocks", the slumps, the adjustments experienced by novice language teachers so that we can provide future trainees with the knowledge and the means to be able to succeed in their first year. This is one of the main purposes of this book: to provide more insights into novice ESL teachers' "ways of knowing," that can be operationalized as blueprints of sorts or set standards for future ESL teacher education programs in many different contexts. It is my belief that pre-service ESL teachers and other novice ESL teachers, regardless of the context they are teaching in, will benefit from knowing that they are not alone when trying to navigate the complex transition from their teacher education programs to their first year as teachers. With such information hopefully more novice teachers will experience a successful and rewarding transition and continue to be caring language teachers for many years to come.

## Conclusion

This chapter has outlined and discussed the reality that many novice teachers face in their first year of teaching in a real school with real students and real classrooms, and with new colleagues. For many novice teachers the transition from their teacher education program to this professional world is a "shock." Some never really recover from this shock, at great personal cost and immense cost to the institutions and governments who have trained them. Some of the reasons for such a "shock" include inadequacies in their training programs as well as factors in the schools where they begin their careers. Several novice teachers feel they have not been adequately prepared for the issues and challenges they must face during their first year, and research in general education in many countries agrees with these novice teachers' perceptions. The conclusion is that teacher educators should become more familiar with the specific issues and challenges that novice teachers will face in their first year, and feed this information back into their teacher education programs so that their pre-service teachers can be better prepared. What is astonishing in the TESOL profession is that there is little information about novice teachers' real experiences during their first year, and this book is one attempt at providing such information.

# Chapter 4

# "The First Week Is Like You're in a Swamp": Developing Awareness

## Introduction

In this and the next four chapters I outline the various experiences, including the shocks, slumps, adjustments and awareness development (this chapter) that the three novice ESL teachers reported about in the twelve group discussions. As mentioned earlier, the order of this presentation of information is not necessarily in terms of the most frequently referenced topics/issues talked about during the group meetings. Rather, chapters 4 through 8 are ordered chronologically in terms of when the topics/issues came up during the teachers' first semester. In this way I am trying to convey a more realistic view of what the three novice ESL teachers experienced as the events occurred from the day they entered the school for the first time. You will remember that I began in chapter 1 by using some of the quotes that appear again in this chapter (but in more contextual detail) as a means of introducing the real issues that novice teachers face to prove the point that we are a profession that still seems to eat its young.

In what follows, readers will find more detailed discussion of these issues from the perspective of the three ESL novice teachers, as well as more about the context to the specific issues and quotes introduced in chapter 1. Specifically, this chapter outlines the three novice teachers' perceptions of themselves from their first day when they walked into the school (and even before that during their job interviews) to the final week of their first semester, as expressed during the group meetings. These discussions included the various insights they each had about themselves as language teachers and their teaching style, personality and character. They also talked about how they became aware of their growth and how they perceived they had developed during their first semester as teachers. In many instances they also reflected on their awareness of their personal goals related to teaching for now and the future, and included issues such as their professional development goals, goals for a course, a class or a lesson (e.g., talking less, talking more, being firmer or being more lenient in class). This chapter discusses these issues in detail.

> ### Reflective Break
>
> - What were your experiences during your first day, and first week in your new school?
> - If you have not started to teach yet, what do you expect on your first day and first week as a novice teacher?
> - Why do you think one teacher said it was like being in a swamp when they arrived in their new school?

## First Shocks

As discussed in the previous chapter, research from many different contexts on the transition novice teachers (and novices in many other professions as well) make from training programs to their first year of practice may result in some kind of shock, be it in terms of culture, praxis or otherwise. The second group meeting discussions with the three novice ESL teachers, which occurred about a week after they had begun teaching, revealed just how soon they had experienced their first shocks. In fact, these shocks happened on the very first day and all through their first week as each novice teacher reported that she had not felt welcome from the very first day. As T3 remarked, "It's not welcoming. You don't feel like, 'Hey come on in. Thanks for joining the team. This is what's going on.' You have to find out a lot of things for yourself." T3 said that she felt that she was "thrown in" and had to figure it all out by herself if she was to survive: "You're just thrown in to survive yourself."

This is a similar feeling to what many other novice teachers experience, as reported in many diverse contexts in the previous chapter, but the three novice ESL teachers in this school were not even introduced to the other teachers when they arrived for their first day at work. T2 stated: "I don't know who the [other] teachers are because I have not been introduced. None of us were introduced." She also said that in order to figure out what to do she tried to listen to what other teachers were saying and pick up information. For the most part, she agreed with T3: "I was becoming aware of similar feelings in being not welcome from the first day …. I overheard someone say: 'Oh this is what's going on.' Yeah, it's definitely not a welcoming experience." T1 noted that when she was asked by someone in her family about her perceptions of the environment after her first week at the school, she said she "felt completely lost." She continued: "Everybody is trying to figure out where they each fit in, because they all seem to be coming and going."

### Reflective Break

- How were you "welcomed" into your new school on your first day/ in your first week?
- If you have not started yet, how do you expect to be welcomed?
- What is your understanding of T3's comment: "You're just thrown in to survive yourself"?
- Did you feel the same way on your first day/in your first week?
- Why would a novice teacher "feel lost" in the first days?
- What can novice teachers do to counteract feeling lost or feeling left alone to survive?
- What can the school and the administration do to make novice teachers feel welcome?

## Aftershocks

Thus, all three novice teachers, from their very first day, experienced the same feelings of alienation: they did not feel welcomed and they realized that they would have to discover everything by themselves if they were to survive their first semester. T1 observed: "The first week I felt like I was brand new because I was experiencing everything for the first time, and so it would have been nice to have some more guidance." Of course, all three novice teachers would experience many further shocks during this first semester.

One of these shocks occurred early in the first week for T1, when the textbook she had been told she was to use in one of her classes was suddenly changed, and moreover nobody had a copy of the new textbook because it had not arrived at that time. T1 felt exasperated because when she had been informed that she was hired and what courses she would be teaching, she was also given a textbook so she could prepare in advance. T1 reflected: "Then on arrival I was told to use a different book than what I was given before, and they didn't even have it." She had made different lesson plans based on the previous book she was told they were going to use. T1 continued: "I was shocked that they suddenly changed the book and also frustrated because they did not even have it and what was I going to do then with no book?" She said that she had had to ask the authorities (or "nag them") for the new book each day of her first week before she finally got it at the end of the week. As T1 noted: "It took me a week of nagging such as asking: 'Where's my book? Where's my book?' Friday the book shows up." With that, she informed her supervisor that she could only begin preparation of new lesson plans based on this new book from the following week, which situated her "uncomfortably behind in lesson planning."

T2 noted that she got a shock when she realized she had not received any password to get access to a particular program all the teachers and students used at that school. She wondered what she should do, especially regarding class lists. T2 said: "I haven't got on to it because I have no password yet so I don't know what to do." She remarked that she was given hard-copy class lists but then realized that she would have to input all the student names and numbers into computer files: "All the teachers are expected to do the administrative work. I don't understand why the class list with their student numbers cannot be sent to us electronically, so we can add [to them], but it's not. We have to do that work ourselves." T3 remarked that her attendance sheets were not even correct: "My attendance sheets are a disaster ... all messed up, too, because they had students missing. It's ridiculous especially since they use a good computer program anyway."

Yet another of what I call "aftershocks" occurred during the first week for T3. When she walked into her classroom for the first time, she said that she "just stood in shock at the crowded classroom." T3 reflected on this moment: "I think I just had no clue about the class size because I was expecting to work with 10 or 12 students and it didn't occur to me that it would be 24 or 25. Oh wow, this is a lot of people." The other two novice teachers also remarked that even though they were expecting to have a lot of students, when they first entered the classroom they too felt a bit overwhelmed with the "full room." T2 noted: "When I actually walked into the classroom I was a bit surprised with the full room because I was completely surrounded with students so I had to take a moment to gather myself."

To compound these shocks and aftershocks all three teachers noted that they did not know who they should talk to for guidance. T3 mentioned this when she said that one reason she did not know the other teachers in the school was that a staff meeting planned for the first week was suddenly cancelled without explanation (as it turned out, they did not have any staff meeting their first semester). As T3 said: "We haven't even had a staff meeting yet [because it was cancelled], so we don't even know all the teachers." To which T1 responded: "It would be nice to meet, you know 'Hi. My name is ... and I teach ....'"

This issue of whom they could address their questions to become even more acute when mid-term examinations approached and none of the three novice teachers knew what was going on or going to happen regarding the exams. T3 continued on the previous theme of having no staff meetings; now she felt a bit of panic as there were still no meetings where she could discuss these exams. She remarked: "I don't know what I'm going to have to do at mid-term. We haven't had a meeting yet with the staff. I thought that the exams were for the whole week, so my mistake." T1 responded that she had overheard from other teachers (this was how they "received" their communications in the school) that the mid-terms would be the following week. Then T3 began to worry more about the exam; she said:

> I have not prepared my mid-term exam yet, which is now happening next week, although I have it in my mind what I want them to do. But no one has said to me, "You have to hand in your mid-terms for us to preview" or "We need them by this date."

Indeed, all three novice teachers noted in the last week of their first semester that they had still not had a single staff meeting. T3 reflected: "We did not have a meeting even about mid-terms, so I don't even know what to do with marks actually. I don't know where to send them." To which T2 added her opinion that these meetings are very important for her to talk about particular issues and get some guidance. She continued: "These are not little things because they make your life impossible. There is probably no point now in having a meeting during the last week." To which T1 added with a laugh: "Maybe next semester if we all get hired back we'll have a meeting." At this, the other two teachers laughed but also rolled their eyes.

## Reflective Break

- What would you have done if the textbook you thought you were going to use was suddenly changed during the first week of classes?
- What would you have done if you had no computer password or no class lists during your first week?
- Who should novice teachers approach in their new school if they have questions to ask?
- Who would/did you approach or who will you approach?
- Why do you think the three novice teachers did not know whom to approach to ask their questions?
- Is it common not to have regular staff meetings in a school?
- Why do you think they did not have any staff meetings?

## Evolving Awareness

The above initial experiences may have left the three novice teachers reeling a bit in their first semester, but they soon realized that in order to survive in their new school environment they would have to come up with some strategies as they gained more awareness through their experiences. Of course, having a group of three like-minded novice teachers reflect on these experiences (with this facilitator) probably helped them a lot when considering what to do about particular issues that arose. That said, as the semester progressed all three teachers felt that they were growing as ESL teachers. At the end of the first semester, T2 noted that because of all they had experienced and all they "had to endure without much guidance," they were growing "into more well-rounded and confident teachers."

During their first semester all three teachers reflected on their awareness of their needs, but at the same time they also worried about how demanding they might seem to the other teachers. For example, T2 observed that she realized she should collaborate with the other teachers in the school, especially when producing her weekly lesson plans, but at the same time she noted that she wanted to teach what she considered important and in her own way. T2 said: "I don't mind collaborating for the purpose of expressing ideas, but I don't want to be the teacher next door. I want to be me, and I want to do my style." T2 remarked that one reason for her insistence that she should be free to follow her ideas and teaching style was because of what she had learned in her teacher education program and courses: "That's what I went to school for. I didn't go to school to follow someone else's lesson plans; otherwise, why did I spend so much time developing my style." (Chapter 8 discusses teaching style in more detail.)

T1 remarked that her awareness was not only restricted to her lesson planning but as a result of being left alone to survive her first semester she has become more aware of what she was doing inside and outside the classroom. She said that now she is more aware of what teaching really is, and it is different than what she thought it was when she first entered the classroom a few weeks earlier. T1 reflected:

> It is not everything you thought it was going to be, especially as, like you said, you are getting paid for teaching hours but when you actually break it down to prep and stuff, it's not much. I could go back to my old job and make more money than what I'm doing right now and have less stress, but I enjoy teaching.

Towards the end of her first semester as a novice teacher T1 said that she was forced to become more aware of what was happening to her and this awareness became even more apparent to her during the novice teacher group discussions. T1 reflected on the difference between where she had been in her first week and where she had arrived in the final week of her first semester. She noted: "The first week felt frenzied because, you know, students were coming, students weren't coming, like lots of that kind of switching around, a lot of testing, and just feeling orientated." T1 said that during this first week she felt as if she was in a swamp: "The first week is like you're in a swamp." To which T3 said: "Yeah, exactly. Like you were on thin ice because you're figuring out what's going on, and then this week is like, okay we're into the deep water now, and it is kind of sink or swim." T3 then noted that in order not to sink they would each have to do something about the all the shocks they were experiencing both inside and outside the classroom.

## Reflective Break

- What does the comment: "okay we're into the deep water now, and it is kind of sink or swim" mean to you?
- "The first week is like you're in a swamp." What is your understanding of this statement?
- Did you have similar feelings or experiences during your first week?
- Do you agree or disagree that these comments above show that the three ESL teachers are beginning to develop some kind of awareness of what they are experiencing? Give reasons for your answer.

## Evolving Awareness of the Classroom

As the semester progressed, all three novice teachers realized that if they wanted to survive they would have to come to terms with their new reality and develop awareness of what was really happening so that they could develop more coping strategies. This development of awareness about classroom issues became more apparent as the group discussions continued during the semester.

For example, as the semester proceeded, T2 noted that she was becoming stricter with her students than she was at the beginning of the semester, because she said that she had reached a point with one class where she was not going to put up with any more students coming late because this was "throwing my lesson plans way off" and her students were falling behind schedule. T2 remarked:

I'm getting tougher on them this week. I have had enough. Monday was the breaking point. My class started at 10 o'clock. At 10:30 am, I had the class there because they just kept trickling in, so at the end of the class, I was off my lesson plan anyway, so we were a little bit behind.

T2 then said that she would now give the latecomers homework to complete, and this would be for marks rather than just show; if they did not do the homework, then they would lose marks. T2 continued: "I said, 'Okay, you're working on something. I want two of these now for homework.' 'What?' they said. Then I said, 'Yeah, you're doing homework and you're getting homework marks. I want to see it tomorrow.'"

T2 said that she told her students that she was fed up with some of them coming in late all the time, and that they were falling behind the other classes as a result. T2 said she felt she needed to explain carefully why she was doing what she was doing, so she told them:

> "Because half the class came in late and we're behind what we need to be doing. You can blame it on the students who are late. You all have homework tonight." Then I said, "I keep warning you guys, and everybody comes in late and you're disturbing my teaching."

T2 realized that she may have waited too long this semester to make these rules but she said she had not expected this to happen. The following semester she would be not be so easy, she said: "This semester I learned some stuff. I'll be a tougher teacher next semester."

T2 said that one way she could develop as a novice teacher was to teach the same course twice so she could learn from teaching it one time and possibly change the way she approached the class now that she had some experience. T2 said: "I would like to teach twice the same and then do something else. Then you can always go back into your old lesson plans and revise."

T1 also had the same idea: "I would like to teach the same things next semester to make it better. I hope that I can learn something from it and if I have the chance to do this class again and make some changes in it." T1 also suggested that she would change her identity a bit the following semester, and noted: "I'll be a tougher teacher next semester. I'm nice now, not too nice, but I think, I learned a lesson. I think I might just be a little bit stricter with some of the requirements but it depends on what class I'm teaching."

T3 also noted that she may be changing as a teacher from her experiences during her first semester as an ESL teacher. She said:

I found that after my first term of teaching ever, I was a lot more lenient than I am willing to be now. Maybe they need that eighth email to kind of remind them, and then I found myself being overwhelmed. So, why should I be overwhelmed when I am trying to do them a favor?

T3 said that she would like to change some of the material she uses in her classes because it was not exciting for her as she could not be a creative teacher. She said: "I'm finding the material dry. There is so much to pack in, and we have to use the textbook. And I don't have time to be creative, nor do I have space to be creative because I have too many students." However, T2 disagreed with T3 about creativity and not following the textbook, as she said her students got frustrated if she did not follow the textbook. T2 observed: "You can't always be creative because the students actually get frustrated with you for not using the textbooks because they paid for them." T1 seemed to agree that because the students "paid a lot of money for their textbooks, then teachers should use them."

## Reflective Break

- Did these three teachers have realistic views about what to expect in terms of class size?
- Why do you think these teachers began to take more control of their teaching?
- Why do you think they were lenient with their students at the beginning but stricter with them as the semester continued?
- Did you have similar experiences?

## Evolving Awareness of the Environment

As the semester progressed, all three novice teachers also began to acquire awareness of their new professional environment and culture. For example, they began to take more notice of their interactions with their colleagues and their work conditions including their workload and pay, and especially the differences in pay between the full-time instructors and themselves as part-time, sessional teachers. For example, when discussing workload, they noted that the teachers who work full-time get paid for time not teaching in a classroom, while they only get paid for the time they teach in a classroom because they are considered part-time, sessional teachers (they have contracts for one session/semester). T3, for example, said that the full-time teachers work from 8 am to 4 pm and get paid for all that time regardless of class teaching time. She continued:

> So they're there, and they are being paid for hours that they are there, while we are being paid for hours that we're teaching, but obviously we have to put in a lot of hours, too, preparing, that are not paid, and yet, we're all in the same mix together.

The three novice teachers then discussed how the full-time teachers also get benefits, which they do not. As T3 expressed it: "I feel like if I was in a different category, [otherwise] I would not be angry about putting in so much extra time." To which T2 responded: "One-year contracts that keep getting renewed. It's not sessional. It's contracts without benefits." This then led to a discussion about pay, where all three novice teachers felt that they did not get paid enough to do all the work associated with teaching, which they found a bit discouraging because of all the preparation time they put in. For example, T1 said that she had heard that:

> For every hour of class you should be putting in two hours of prep and marking time and this is especially for us novice teachers. So this leaves you working nine hours a day of teacher working time. This doesn't include lunch of breaks and works out to around \$X/hour. Welcome to the exciting career of being an ESL teacher.

T3 then pointed out why being full-time would be an advantage because they could prepare when they were not teaching but still get paid for this time:

> If I was there for the whole day and I had four hours of teaching and then I had the other hours for prep time, then I would absolutely be willing to sit down with everybody and talk about teaching and the like, and I'm being paid for being there the whole day.

T3 also said that she does not teach just for the money, but at the same time she does not want to be taken advantage of, especially if asked to volunteer her time:

> I'm not only working for the compensation only, but realistically, if I am not being compensated, I should not be expected to do anything else when there are able-bodied people who are already paid to be there. They should be doing it. I like to volunteer when I choose to volunteer. That's what volunteering is.

### Reflective Break

- What working conditions and pay do you expect to obtain for your first year as a novice ESL teacher?
- What will you do if you discover that your pay lags behind all the other teachers in your school?
- T3 had issues about not being compensated for volunteering. What are your expectations regarding volunteering when you are a novice teacher? Do you expect to be compensated for volunteering?
- Do you think institutions take unfair advantage of novice teachers by asking them to do lots more than teach in their novice year?
- Do you think the fact that they were participants in a novice teacher reflection group helped them become more aware of their needs than if they were left alone to experience these issues?
- What do you think may have occurred if these teachers were not members of a teacher reflection group?
- What would you do if you experienced these issues and you were alone?

## Emerging from the Swamp

As the above accounts of the three novice teachers' experiences during their first weeks indicate, they were well immersed in what Donald Schön (1983: 42) has called the "swampy lowlands" of teaching in real classrooms "where situations are confusing 'messes.'" Perhaps all teachers need to experience these swampy lowlands at some point in their career, in order to be able to gain insight and awareness so that they can move on from the swamp. It seems that all three novice teachers gained some insights from their experiences (although they were left alone to struggle within that swamp and could very well have been completely submerged).

For example, T1 reflected on her emergence from the swamp as she talked about her realization near the end of her first semester that actually she did not know as much about teaching as she thought she did at the beginning of the semester; she remarked: "Being a teacher, the more I know, the more I realize I don't know." T1 said that this realization was not a sudden one but "emerged slowly during the semester" in her classes, especially when her students asked her questions about what she was teaching and she sometimes had a hard time finding the correct response for each question. T1 remarked: "Every day I feel, 'Oh gee that was a great point or a great question' and I wish I could come up to a better answer on the spot." T1 also said that she was beginning to look at her students' learning more at the end of the semester rather than just her own survival. She observed: "As the semester was winding down I wondered more about their learning and I think I discovered the importance of being spontaneous in class rather than stopping to think too much to make a point or answer a question, otherwise I will lose my students' attention." T1 continued: "Being spontaneous, I think, is very important—not spontaneous in preparation, but spontaneous in delivery because this helps to hold students' attention."

T2 also noted that she was worried her lessons would be perceived as boring if she was not always ready to keep the dialogue going. T2 said: "If you're just there to, to drill the knowledge into their heads, it's going to make it so boring." T2 suggested an idea to the others that perhaps, now that they had become more aware of what they was happening in their lessons and the school to some extent, they should consider teaching the same classes the following semester so that they could be better. T2 remarked: "I was thinking that I would like to teach the same things next semester to make it better and you can reflect on your style and your comfort a little more."

Fuller & Brown (1975) describe two general stages of developmental challenges for novice teachers. The first stage is characterized by survival and mastery while the second stage presents an either/or dichotomy of development: either settling into a state of resistance to change or staying open to adaptation and change in their practice. In the early stage, novice teachers are most concerned about their own survival as teachers. Novice teachers' idealized concerns (the ideal of teaching before experiencing the reality of teaching) are abruptly replaced by concerns about their own survival. They are also concerned about control of the class (classroom management) and the content of their instruction. In the later stage, novice teachers become more concerned about their teaching performance, and this includes noticing their perceived limitations and frustrations in the teaching context. After this stage, but much later on in the first year, as Fuller & Brown (1975) argue, novice teachers become more concerned about their students' learning and the impact of their teaching on this learning. The two teachers' reflections above, on their development from a survival and mastery stage to where they become more focused on their students' learning and the impact of their teaching on learning, indicate that they seem to be progressing according to Fuller & Brown's (1975) stages.

### Reflective Break

- All three teachers were required to perform some additional tasks and roles during their first semester, most of which were unpaid. Do you think this is normal practice in most schools?
- Do you think you will be asked to do similar tasks and roles and if so, how will you respond?
- Have you had similar experiences with these tasks and roles, and how did you respond?
- Why do you think that insight and awareness took time and was a slow process for all three novice teachers?
- What can schools do to help novice teachers overcome some of the issues outlined above so that awareness and insight can be enhanced?
- What can teacher education programs do to help novice teachers overcome some of the issues outlined above so that awareness and insight can be enhanced?
- What can other teachers do to help novice teachers overcome some of the issues outlined above so that awareness and insight can be enhanced?

## Conclusion

This chapter has pointed out the problems that all three novice ESL teachers encountered from their very first day in school, which they had to find ways to deal with if they were to survive. They said that they did not feel very welcome and that they were left to fend for themselves. All three novice teachers talked about a lack of communication in their new environment and that they felt confused when it came to certain procedures both inside and outside the classroom because nobody gave them any instructions about what to do. They did not know departmental procedures because they were new, and were confused about how to proceed with certain things like mid-terms and changes in textbooks. In addition, they said that they did not know whom to ask about the problems they were encountering and that they felt like they were in a swamp. Some of the problems they encountered included being able to find the time to do all the work a teacher must do, how to deal with problems that make it hard to teach a class, such as large class sizes and boring required teaching material. However, rather than giving up, all three teachers slowly realized that they were in a sink-or-swim situation and that it was up to each of them to be able to understand what was happening if they were to survive this first semester. As the semester progressed, the novice teachers began to take more responsibility for their own development and more control of their teaching, regardless of the fact that they had no real mentorship in the school. All three teachers even discussed how they would want to improve how they teach in the following semester and build on what they had done before. They all wanted to use what they had experienced and learned during their first semester and continue to grow into more well-rounded and confident teachers in the future. The next chapter discusses in more detail some of the issues that have been briefly outlined here.

# Chapter 5

# "Here's the Book, Go Teach": Managing the Classroom

## Introduction

Of the many different issues the novice ESL teachers discussed during their group meetings, the topic they talked about the most was their approaches and methods. In fact this subject accounted for more than 60 per cent of all the comments made by the novice teachers. This chapter deals with what the teachers talked about at the group meetings in terms of their approaches and methods. The chapter outlines how the novice teachers described their personal theories of their approaches and methods and how these were impacted by the context in which they were teaching, such as the school administration and their colleagues. In addition, the chapter also includes a discussion of the impact of their students on their teaching approaches and methods. We begin with an overall discussion of their initial experiences with the school administration as this sets the scene for what was later to happen regarding their approaches and methods.

## The School Administration

Regarding the administration all three novice teachers have plenty to say and most of the comments reveal that they were confused throughout their first semester because when they did get any signals from the administration, these were mostly mixed. All three novice teachers acknowledged that when they first arrived at the school they heard that the administration would allow them to be creative in terms of how they could teach the prescribed curriculum and go through the textbook; and although they were required to produce weekly lesson plans for inspection, they heard they could also be creative with these. However, soon after they started to actually teach, they said that they realized that from a general perspective the administration seemed to be disorganized and this (disorganization) was especially frustrating for them because, as they were novice teachers, it tended to cause uncertainty which in turn led them sometimes to doubt their teaching.

For example, T1 noted that before the first week she thought the administration was "Not too controlling and allows for some freedom in planning and teaching an ESL class." T1 said that she thought this because she had been instructed to make daily lesson plans and submit these to the coordinator of the particular level she was teaching. T1 said that this sounded good to her because as a novice she thought there was "a sense of accountability, but also a sense of freedom to make my own lesson plans." T1 thought that because she was required to hand in her lesson plan each week, this in turn encouraged her to plan ahead and be ready to teach a particular class on a given day. She said that she was excited about this whole process before she began teaching because it made her think about her classes and she hoped too that this would generate discussions and collaboration with other teachers about what they were about to teach. As T1 noted:

> Because you're working with a coordinator every week submitting your lessons, and you have your long-term plan and your short-term plan, and you're on track. I feel like if you need the support of somebody above you, you have it. That's what I mean by accountable. We can talk to other teachers as well about what we are doing.

T2 agreed as she noted that, because they were novice teachers and had so much going on each day which they had never experienced before, if they had not been required to make such plans, they would not have done so: "I'm pleased with that. I feel like … if I'm not made to do those things then I likely won't."

So, although the coordinators required the teachers to make these lesson plans, novice teachers welcomed this as well as the general idea of knowing that they had someone to go to if they had any questions. This was especially important for these teachers because they had not taught in such a school before and had not seen the books that were being used at each level. In addition, all three said that they were told they would be asked about their opinions of the book and the materials they were using for a particular level at the end of the semester. As T3 remarked: "They've said: 'Tell me what you think of the book after the semester.'" All in all, the three novice teachers seemed pleased with the administration before their first week of teaching; they were eager to prepare daily lesson plans and hand them in to the relevant coordinators for feedback, and were willing to talk to other teachers about their lesson plans whenever they would get a chance.

> ### Reflective Break
>
> - Were you, like these three novice teachers, excited before you started to teach even though you would be required to make daily lesson plans and hand them in for feedback?
> - Do you think teachers, and especially novice teachers, should be required to make term plans and daily lesson plans? Why, or why not?
> - What would you expect to include in a term plan?
> - What would you expect to include in a daily lesson plan?
> - Would you expect to get some guidance about what you would be teaching in a school when you first start?
> - If you answer yes to the question above, who do you think will give you this guidance?
> - If you answer no to the first question above, how will you cope with lessons in your first semester?

## "Here's the Book, Go Teach!"

From the comments above it seems that all three novice teachers were happy with their initial impressions of what was required of them when they first entered the school. However, when they started to teach on the first day, they said that they began to notice some disorganization in how things actually operated. For example, T2 said that she did not know the school used a particular textbook until she arrived the first day to teach, as she was not informed about this during her interview for the job. In fact, during her interview, she said that she was not informed about anything related to teaching or who exactly she would be teaching, and she said she was afraid to ask at that time.

Then on her first day of teaching, T2 said, another teacher (she cannot remember who because she said it was all a blur after one hour) instructed her: "Here's the book, go teach!" T2 said that this was the extent of her orientation and introduction to teaching in her first week: she was not given any real instructions about what to do, or any induction into how the classes would unfold, how the school operated or any other advice on how to go about her teaching.

During the second week, when she returned to submit her required long-term lesson plan, T2 said she was told that there was to be another different book for the particular course she was teaching, but they did not have it in stock yet. She recounted that when she handed in her long-term learning plan:

> The coordinator said, "Oh, there's another book." Then I said, "You're kidding, right?" And she said, "No." I said, "Where is it?" And she said, "I don't have it yet." So I said, "What do I do?"

T2 said that she did not get a reply to her last question, as the coordinator had no answer, and so she felt a sense of panic, disorientation and frustration all at the same time.

This sense of isolation and frustration only increased as their first term progressed, as all three teachers noted that by the fifth week, they had not had any meetings with any other teachers, coordinators or the administration and were left to their own devices to "figure out things by themselves" (T2). For instance, they said that as the weeks went by during their first semester they did not know about how examinations were to be structured, or by whom, and who would implement them. Then as the mid-term exam time approached (as written in the syllabus they were given at the beginning of the semester) they began to panic; As T3 remarked,

> I have not prepared my mid-term exam yet, which is happening next week although I have it in my mind what I want them to do. But no one has said to me, "You have to hand in your mid-terms for us to preview" or "We need them by this date" or whatever. We haven't had a meeting yet, ever.

In agreement, T1 said that while she perceived that her classes were working well, she did not know whom to talk to about the exam system that she was confused about but that she was supposed to follow. She stated: "I am very frustrated when it comes to making exams because accordingly we have to submit an exam."

## Reflective Break

- What would you have done if you were told: "Here's the book, go teach"?
- Do you think novice teachers should be mentored about how to use a book for a level they are about to teach, or should they be able to decide how to use it themselves?
- What would you do if someone told you that another book was prescribed for a particular class but it had not arrived at the school yet?

> - Do you think a novice teacher should make his or her own exam for the class he or she is teaching, or should he or she ask a more experienced teacher who is teaching the same level for help in making the exam?
> - How would you handle a situation where you did not know what to do about an approaching mid-term exam?

## Taking the Initiative

In the previous chapter I pointed out that the teachers' sense of awareness began to evolve during their very first week because they realized they were in a sink-or-swim type situation, left to themselves to determine which one (sink or swim) it would become during their first semester. As their sense of awareness began to evolve at this time, so too did their realization that they would have to take the initiative (their own) in order to survive in that school.

All three novice teachers were becoming aware of their sense of frustration about who (and when) they could communicate with about their classes, even though they had a coordinator in place at each level they were teaching. They wondered, for example, about how to use their books (if they had them) and about how to prepare for the mid-term examinations (that were fast approaching). The three teachers said they realized (through various discussions during the group meetings) that they would have to take care of things themselves and as a result they decided to take the initiative to make sure things got done in their classes. As their first term progressed, they said they began to feel more distant from the other teachers; they did not feel a part of the group of established and more experienced teachers. As T3 noted: "You don't feel like: 'Hey come on in. Thanks for joining the team. This is what's going on.' You have to find out a lot of things for yourself."

They realized that they would have to take the initiative when it came to connecting their lesson plans (that were to be submitted weekly) and the content of the mid-term exams. Even though all three novices mentioned that when they first heard about the idea of making lesson plans and submitting them to the coordinator they liked this, nevertheless as the term progressed they said that they also found this process could be frustrating and this really surfaced when the time came to make the mid-term exams. For example, T1 said that she was unsure about how to deal with her experienced colleagues when they disagreed over the exam content that she submitted to her group. As T1 noted earlier, her class did not have a book for some time and as a result she had given them magazine articles to read.

She wanted to include these in the mid-term exam but her more experienced colleague disagreed. T1 said: "My experienced colleague just felt that the magazine articles would not be suitable for the exam, but that's what they had been reading for the last month. We hadn't even used the textbook for the last month."

T1 said that she felt frustrated and insulted by this because she had included those magazine articles in her lesson plans some time back and had submitted all these to the coordinator and all the teachers who were teaching that particular level. She felt frustrated with the whole process of submitting lesson plans because she said she now began to realize that nobody read them. She continued:

> [This was] a little bit of an insult. I thought, well, do you actually know what I've been teaching, then? Here I've spent all this time making sure you get my lesson plans, thinking that it's for you to also give me feedback if you think I'm going off track. I hadn't received anything back until the exam. So that kind of bothered me a bit.

T2 also said that she found submitting lesson plans to coordinators and to other teachers a bit disorganized and confusing sometimes. The coordinators seemed to be going week-by-week merely in reaction to things rather than with any real planning in mind. T2 said she noticed this when she took the initiative and prepared her mid-term listening exams well in time, and this seemed to remind the coordinator to ask the other teachers to do the same:

> I told the coordinator, "Next week I'll bring you my Listening Exam," and she said, "Well, they are not due for another two weeks." I said, "Listen. If I'm not going to submit them, I'll forget because I have final exams there." So I brought it, and she said, "Oh good. Now I know that I have to ask everybody else for their Listening Exams, so thank you for keeping me in line."

The teachers also talked about how they interacted with their colleagues. They said that sometimes this was good but then they would feel frustrated because the administration in the form of coordinators did not want to acknowledge what they had collaborated on. This happened when T3 collaborated with another colleague (outside the group under discussion in this book) who was teaching the same level to make an exam based on what they had produced in their lesson plans and had executed in their reading classes. When they had finished preparing the exam which was based on their students' reading magazine articles during the semester (as described above), they had to submit it to that level coordinator for approval but it was rejected. T3 reflected:

> After we submitted the exam, which we thought was pretty good, it was sent back almost immediately saying, "No. This is too difficult. It's full of colloquialism, and even a native speaker wouldn't understand it," at which I was a little surprised.

T3 said that she felt frustrated with this decision as did the other teacher, because they knew their students were familiar with the material in the exam they had prepared. However, even though T3 disagreed, she decided not to contest the decision because she was a new teacher. She noted that what happened in the end was that they used one of the exams that was approved "a couple of years ago" and, as T3 remarked, "it kind of bothered me that if she's the coordinator who has read our lesson plans all along, would she not know that we thought that this exam was appropriate for the class?"

T3 was said that she was willing to concede that as a novice teacher she did not have as much experience as the coordinator; however, she said the coordinator should have communicated some feedback earlier to her so that she would have known more clearly what to do. T3 reflected: "Maybe part of it was that we are new and I'm willing to take advice, but I think she wanted to find something wrong because there had been no feedback before."

An interesting point that was revealed during the group meetings was that the three novice teachers did not talk much to each other about their teaching methods. When they did comment on their teaching methods, they said that they were most interested in using methods, approaches and material that could make their lessons interesting for the students. They felt that if their approaches and methods were interesting, their students would learn better and pay more attention. They said that they had to be aware of the possibility of lessons becoming boring for their students because they felt constrained by the textbooks that they were required to use which were restricting what they thought they could do in class. As a result the teachers agreed that they would try to bring examples from the students' daily lives into their lessons. This is discussed in more detail in the section that follows.

### Reflective Break

- What would you have done if the coordinator had rejected your mid-term exam even though it reflected what you and other colleagues covered in your classes?

- Do you think more experienced teachers do not take novice teachers seriously and think they do not know much about teaching?
- Why do you think the three novice teachers in this group did not talk much about their teaching methods to each other?
- Do you think that teachers generally are willing to talk about their teaching methods to their colleagues? Why, or why not?

## Making Lessons Work

Part of the three teachers taking the initiative was that they decided that they would be responsible for making their lessons work. They talked a lot about how they wanted their materials, approach and lessons to be interesting for the students. All three novice teachers were of the same opinion, that if their approaches and methods were interesting to their students, then those students would learn better and pay more attention in class. Thus they suggested that if they could make their students' learning experience in class more interesting and enjoyable, they would become successful teachers. They all had different ways of making their lessons interesting.

For example, T2 said that in order to make her lessons interesting she would have to add more to each lesson than only using the book; so she said she decided that she would "supplement the book." T2 continued: "I can't really stand the books that I teach here. So I supplement them because the textbook usually is boring." To do this she said that she brought in more real-world materials that would raise greater interest among her students. She said her choice of these materials depended on what the lesson focus of that day was.

T1 agreed and mentioned that she tried to use everyday examples from her students' lives. She explained: "I always use examples of the students themselves in the class because, first of all, you're always interested in yourself." T1 also said she used Canadian comedy from TV shows to make her classes interesting: "Today we watched an episode of *Corner Gas*, which is a Canadian comedy. And they had to choose what they were going to critique, because the unit is movie, movie critiquing. So critique the plot storyline or critique the characters."

Although the novice teachers said that at first they had a difficult time deciding on how they could make their lessons interesting considering that they had to cover specific chapters from their required textbooks, towards the end of their first semester all three of them believed that they had a better understanding of how to make their lessons work and what methods worked with which groups of students in their classes. T3, for example, noted that she became more experimental in her teaching approaches and methods with various classes and that she tried out different methods to correct what she intended to do if one particular method did not work out the first time.

T3 went on to explain an example in her writing class when she realized that the grading scheme she had developed at the beginning of the semester was "too generous" and that she needed to adjust all the grades for one particular assignment. For that writing assignment T3 had been giving separate marks for items that were not related to the overall development of a paragraph, such as the length of the paragraph and grammar. As T3 remarked: "I kind of needed to bring their marks down, and I know it sounds bad, but they did really too well on the mid-term. I don't think that's an accurate mark because I gave them 5 marks for length. Their grammar wasn't bad, so they got the marks." As a result, she said, their overall marks were too high and not reflective of their ability to write in English: "Their whole writing is not that great and they're getting 80s because of my marking scheme, but they are not good at putting sentences together in a paragraph." So T3 decided to change her marking methods and "bring their marks down a little bit. I don't want them thinking they're great writers." Although she made these changes, she noted that she was still worried because she realized the students would not be happy with the changes. However, she said that it was "for their own good because if they did not realize their mistakes, they would not be successful writers later." As T3 noted: "They are going to get into a higher level if I let them get away with this [high grades] but they will struggle later too with this. They probably won't be happy that I changed the marks."

T1 said that in her writing classes as the semester went on she began to focus on using examples that students could relate to and enjoy because she said she wanted to maximize learning. To do this she said she developed a way of teaching her students how to paraphrase in a more interesting way. T1 explained:

> I always involve a made-up scandal. So I would put an example on the board. I would write two or three sentences about one of the students that was so ridiculous that nobody could believe it; because you don't want to write something that maybe true because that would be a nightmare and you could get in a lot of trouble. Then I would ask everybody to write, re-write the scandal in their own words. I would say that's paraphrasing.

In addition, when the novice teachers did discuss their methods in the group meetings, they attempted to give advice to each other about methods but sometimes discovered that even though methods may work in one particular class they may not work in another. This happened when the teachers were sharing an idea in the reflective group about getting their students more involved in each class and T1 came up with an idea of trying to get everyone in each class to participate at least once every twenty seconds, to which T3 responded that it would not work for her because her class was emphasizing a different skill. As T3 reflected on T1's idea, she said: "Although that's a good idea, I wouldn't be able to do that in my other class because it's not Speaking, it's a Reading class ... even if it's discussion time it's not to the extent that like twenty seconds someone must speak."

> **Reflective Break**
>
> - The three novice teachers suggested that it was important for all of them to focus on how to make the class interesting for the students. Do you agree with them?
> - If you disagree, explain why.
> - If you think it important to make class interesting, in what ways do you make your approaches and methods interesting for your students?
> - Two of the novice teachers try to make their classes interesting by focusing on using reality in their classes; that is, they want to use real examples for the students because by doing this maybe their students are able to better understand or feel like it applies to them personally. Do you do this? If so, how; if not, why not?

## Dealing with Difficult Learners

When the novice teachers talked in detail about their learners, the discussions mainly focused on their perceptions of how their learners responded to their lesson plans, teaching approaches and methods, and especially on how they could better control their learners during lessons. T1, for example, described how one student was giving her "some trouble" by constantly coming late and not completing his assignments; and when he did come, he continuously interrupted her during class. T1 said that one day she decided to put her homework instructions on the board in writing so this student could see them, because in response to any question about homework, T1 noted that he always said that he did not know about the assignment. So, T1 said, she decided to change her approach to how she gave homework instructions. She continued: "Then one day I put the instruction on the board, I didn't announce it or anything. The next day I said, 'Oh, you were supposed to do it if you were late, and I haven't received anything.'" The student said, as usual: "Oh you didn't tell us," to which T1 replied, "Ah, it was on the board." T1 then continued to explain to her class about coming late and homework requirements, and told them that if they were late then their class participation mark would be adversely impacted:

> The whole point of the late question is so I don't have to keep interrupting the class. If I have to stop and tell you you're late, that interrupts my class .... So now your mark will be affected by your attendance. You guys have known this from the beginning. You get a mark for class participation.

The issue of difficult students was also highlighted by T2 who told the group how one student challenged her openly in class in her first days at the school and that this was a shock because she had only just started teaching. T2 noted that she had just begun the class by asking her students a question and one student answered her in a sarcastic manner: "I asked them a question and I said, 'What do you think?' and one student said to me, 'I don't know. You're the teacher.'" T2 said at the time she was shocked but realized that she had to respond quickly or she would have continuous problems with this student (and probably with the class) in future. So she quickly replied to the student: "Oh, but you are the student. You have to make a decision if you agree with it." Although this seemed to work T2 said that the whole incident caused her to panic for a moment because she had not been expecting any student to react in such a manner. She said that she was shocked at the student's demeanor at the time; T2 reflected: "She looked at me like, 'Well, just tell me if I am right or wrong and be done with it.' I was shocked and wondered how to break that, I don't know." All three novice teachers realized during the group discussions that they were constantly trying to figure out how to control their students' behavior as it occurred and experimenting with different methods of how to do this.

Linked to their concerns about some of their students' behavior during lessons were discussions about the impact of their students' cultural backgrounds and how this may have impacted their classroom behavior. For example, T3 said that when she started teaching for the first time this semester, she had never thought about her students' cultural backgrounds and how this may impact learning and teaching. She said that she only came to realize this point when she was putting students together in a routine manner and asking them to work in groups, and how this turned out to be a complete surprise for her. T3 stated: "I just did the guy-girl thing, I didn't look at ethnicity." Then she explained how she tried to get people from different cultural backgrounds to work together but sometimes it was difficult. T3 reflected: "I tried to put a student from [country X] together with a student from [country Y] but they did not want to work together. They then told me who they wanted to work with and it was usually with someone from their own country." T3 said that she did not know what to do about how to put her students in groups because when she formed mixed groups with members from different countries, she discovered that there were students who "talked all the time and these seemed to be from one particular country only and the other students just remained silent." T3 wondered: "Are the quiet students intimidated by the talkative students or are they happy to let them talk so they don't have to? I am not sure."

T1 and T2 relayed that they too had similar issues when pairing up students from different countries and as a result they said that they decided to allow students from the same cultural backgrounds to stay together when working as a pair or in a group. T1 noted: "I find it difficult to get students from different cultural backgrounds to pair up or work in groups and so I let students from the same cultural group stay together and work as a group because it is easier both for me and for them."

## Reflective Break

- What would you do if one student challenged you openly?
- What would you do if a student continuously interrupted you during class?
- All three novice teachers discussed how their students' cultural backgrounds have an impact on learning and classroom behavior. Do you agree that this can have an impact? If yes, how? If not, why not?
- The three novice teachers mentioned that they had issues when grouping students from different cultural backgrounds. Do you think students from different cultural backgrounds should be made work in groups with students from other cultural backgrounds, or allowed to only work with students from a similar cultural group?
- Given that students are from different cultural backgrounds, should male and female students be asked to work together in pairs or groups regardless of their different cultural backgrounds?
- The three novice teachers all mention situations where they use different methods to "control" their students in the classroom. How would you "control" your students?

## Conclusion

This chapter has presented the three novice teachers' reflections on their various approaches and methods. This is by far the most frequently discussed of the issues and topics they talked about during their first semester. This included what they noted about the actual approaches and methods they used in their teaching and how their learners reacted in different ways. They also talked about the impact of the school context, and in particular the administration, on their teaching, such as the need to produce weekly lesson plans for a prescribed curriculum. They described their approaches and methods in terms of what worked and what did not work in their lessons. In this way they were also able to give advice to each other about approaches and methods.

It seems then that the novice teachers' impressions changed as the weeks passed, starting from the time when they first walked in the door on the first day when they said that they liked being held accountable by the administration while at the same time also enjoying some freedom to plan and teach the way they liked. However, as the semester progressed so too did their level of frustration with the administration, in that they found it unorganized and not very clear in its procedures, which resulted in a feeling of uncertainty and in the novice teachers needing to take extra initiative. As a result all three teachers realized that they would have to act for themselves if they were to survive their first semester. They did this by trying to make their lessons more interesting, supplementing the required textbooks with more relevant materials. They also noted that they would have to come up with their own ways to deal with difficult learners, as they had little guidance from the school administration. The next chapter presents an account of the teachers' self-evaluation: How successful were these methods in the classroom and in encouraging different types of students to learn?

# Chapter 6
# "It Was Very Dry": Evaluating Lessons

## Introduction

In the previous chapter the three novice teachers talked about their approaches and methods (the most frequent topic during all the group discussions) and also how they realized that they would have to take the initiative in making their lessons more interesting and when dealing with difficult learners in order to be able to survive their first semester. In this chapter I outline and discuss how they evaluated their lessons and what overall questions they generated as a result of this reflection. In addition, the chapter presents their perceptions on what they consider to be effective lessons, which include discussions about their accounts of their learners' responses and behavior during lessons.

## Control during Lessons

The main concern for all three novice teachers in terms of lesson evaluation was the issue of control during the lesson. For example, there was a discussion about how worried they all were about keeping (or not losing) control of their classes as they all seemed to have experienced it at one stage or another during their first semester teaching. T1, for example, noted that she felt that she "may have lost control once because the students were not all working with each other. I think they don't like each other." She reflected that when she first went into that class to teach her speaking lesson, her first mistake was that she did not organize the class in any particular way. T1 continued: "The whole place just exploded and everybody started talking at once and nobody listed to me any longer." She remarked that even one of her students noticed what was happening: "One of my students from [country X], he says, 'I don't think they're paying attention to what you're saying.' And I said, 'That's okay. It's Speaking Class.' But I knew it was not okay." T1 reflected on this later while going home, realizing that she must consider how to take more control in her classroom. She said: "As I was on the way home I was thinking about control of the classroom."

T1 brought this topic of control to the teacher reflection group for discussion, but was nervous about sharing that she might actually have lost control and said that maybe she had not lost total control. As T1 noted: "I was thinking about it. I personally didn't feel that I lost control of the classroom though now, once I realized it, I keep it more under control now if I can." T1 then expressed her opinion that a good lesson is one in which she has total control over what happens, and that the students are more unified and they appreciate it when the teacher takes control. She remarked:

> When I take full control, I do feel that they appreciate it more. I don't know why. I love my Level X class. I just wanted to say actually, when we were talking, my Level X class is so unified. It's just a pleasure to teach them.

T3 relayed that she too had issues with lesson control when she first went into her classes in her first semester and especially when she tried to form groups for the first time. She discovered that if she did not control exactly who would sit with whom, it would turn out to be a messy exercise. T3 observed: "When I was trying to form groups, I was trying to do things not knowing who was coming and going and it all turned out very messy until I took over and told them where to sit." Although she told them where to sit, T3 noted that she was not totally comfortable with this, because she had thought that they would form groups quickly and easily but soon discovered this not to be the case. However, after teaching for a few weeks she said she began to take more control of where her students sat during particular lessons and this made her feel better about her lessons because now her students knew what to expect. T3 noted: "I do feel like it's a more successful lesson when the students know what to expect and I feel like I know a little bit more of what I'm doing every week."

T2 said that she faced a similar issue of lack of control to start with in some of her classes, but she decided to change her approach immediately in the second week. She began to take more control of every class regardless of how they responded, as she said that she "did not want to let any complacency develop." T2 noted that her students know now exactly what to do and what to expect in each class because she has preassigned partners for all lessons:

> We can get down to business very quickly. You come in, you sit with your partner. If you miss something, you're away, then it's the

responsibility of your partner to fill you in. It's not my responsibility to re-teach what I taught because you were absent or whatever.

When the other teachers questioned if this was difficult to achieve or if the students would get tired of it, T2 responded: "You don't waste any time. If they complain, you just tell them that it's tough love."

### Reflective Break

- Do you think teachers can and should control their classes at all times?
- Do you think group work helps or hinders classroom control?
- Do you think that when students know what to expect in terms of classroom organization, lessons will run better?
- Do you think pre-assigned partners for activities are a good idea or bad idea for classroom organization? Give reasons for your answer.

## Evaluating Teaching

As the semester continued, the three novice teachers noticed that they were generating lots of questions related to evaluation of their teaching. These questions made them realize that they were still novice and inexperienced teachers. As a result they said that they sometimes felt their teaching was inadequate for their students' learning. T3 said that she had an uncomfortable feeling after teaching the first half of her first semester: she wondered if her students were learning anything during her lessons and whether she was teaching them in the correct way.

T3 said that she got this uncomfortable feeling during one of her lessons in mid-semester when she noticed that many of her students were not responding in her classes. She said that she was faced with a feeling of self-doubt as she evaluated her teaching in those classes. T3 brought this to the attention of the group as she remarked: "I think they're bored, and so I was questioning myself the other day. Am I finding it difficult to get past a certain stage with them because they haven't been taught properly in [the previous Level]? Or, am I not teaching them properly in this Level?" T3 then reflected on what she should really evaluate, her own present teaching or what her students had experienced in their classes the previous semester. She continued: "So, I'm questioning, is it my teaching, or is it some of the teaching they had before?"

T3's evaluations generated a lot of discussion in the group about the place of experience and their prior teacher training and education, and the value of such training to prepare them adequately to be able to handle any teaching situation. As T2 noted, when teachers are given a level or class in an existing program they are placed in a situation in which they have to adapt quickly regardless; and if they have been trained properly, they will be able to do this. She remarked:

> Aren't we always parachuted into a situation and then it's whatever skills we have to handle it. So if we've got the training, then we shouldn't feel parachuted in. We should feel equipped because we're trained.

T1 then suggested that their lack of experience is not that important if they are excited about what they are doing, and that they can overcome any mistakes they make as first-year teachers with this enthusiasm as long as they are disciplined. She said:

> I think the lack of experience is not as important as lack of excitement about what you're doing as a first-year teacher, but you need discipline and not making changes but giving the chance to the students to do the work. Everybody makes mistakes whether you have experience or not.

T2 added that regardless of their teaching experience, teachers must also consider their students' learning style, and reflect on whether their teaching style is well-matched or not with every student's learning style. T2 remarked: "Our teaching style is not always compatible with our students' learning styles. So all teachers must be able to step back and see this or they will get lost teaching." The focus of discussion on this issue of student learning style when evaluating the success of their lessons then shifted to their perceived difficulty of dealing with students who have such different learning styles, because they need extra attention during the lessons (chapter 8 discusses teaching style in more detail).

All three teachers commented that they found it difficult to focus on the whole class during a lesson when they knew that one or two students required a lot more personal and special attention during that lesson. As first-year teachers, they said they were having a difficult time working out how to facilitate all this during their lessons. T1, for example, noted that she had a problem trying to figure out how to deal with a student who seemed to be off task for most of her lessons and, as a result, tended to disrupt the flow of the lessons. T1 said that she especially noted this when the student was required to give a presentation on a specific topic that had been assigned to her, but ended up talking about something completely different when she presented the topic. T1 remarked: "For the presentation, she didn't even do the presentation with, with the, about the right topic. She didn't even talk about her topic." As a result, T1 said, the whole lesson (which was focused on that particular topic) was disrupted because the other students did not know what to do or what questions to ask because they had not prepared anything about the topic that the student presented. T1 then asked the group what she should have done or what she can do in future about such a student.

This generated a lot of discussion in the group. T3 wondered if the reason the student did not do what she was supposed to could be because she wanted to stand out from the other students. T3 remarked: "So is it because she is not allowed to shine? Is that what it is? She needs to shine because some people are like that?"

T2 suggested the possibility that the student was facing some kind of culture shock. She said: "I'm wondering if maybe she's having some culture shock and that's why she's acting out." T1 replied that that could be the case but that she was not really sure what was going on. She added that she thought the student had a high opinion of her own English abilities. T1 said, "I don't know. The problem is that I think the student thinks she's so good." T1 continued that she said she did not want this to happen in her lessons because of the attention these students get: "I don't like it because she steals a lot of attention. I don't like it because it should not be like this."

T3 said that she also wondered how to handle such students who need attention. At the beginning she found that she was trying very hard to include all students: she would contact them outside class to make sure they were following. But now that she was mid-way through the term she had changed. T3 said:

> I found that my first weeks of teaching, I was a lot more lenient than I am willing to be now, and the same thing that you think that you're giving them an opportunity or maybe they just need encouragement, maybe they need that eighth email to kind of remind them, and then I found myself being overwhelmed.

Then she said that she realized that if she always felt overwhelmed she could not help anybody, and she decided not to try too much anymore. T3 remarked: "So, why should I be overwhelmed when I am trying to do them a favor?"

However, this then led a discussion on how they were allowed by the administration to deal with such students in their lessons, especially those students who disrupted the success of their lessons. The novice teachers realized that the "school in which they teach is also a business" (T2). As T2 wondered, if the school slogan is that "it is all about the students" then why are the teachers not allowed to continue following the approach to their lessons which they have worked out as best for their students? T2 wanted to give her students more work to do but was afraid of the students' complaints to the administration, about which she had heard before. T2 remarked: "If it's all about the kids .... We're doing the best for the kids. And I know as a teacher it's not the best for the kids, so that's what is bothering me."

T2 then said that even though she knows some of what is being practiced in the school is not really good for the students in terms of learning English, she also realizes that there is little that she can do because the school is also a business and wants to keep the clients happy. T2 continued: "It's not really for the kids. It's a business. It's for the money, right? It's not always about the student, it's about the profits." The other two novice teachers said that they too felt some pressure in giving the students what they wanted but not necessarily what they needed, and so they said they felt inadequately prepared from their teacher education programs and courses in how to deal with this and other issues in their first year. Their feelings of inadequacy were further manifested when they talked about more specific problems and their proposed solutions—some of which are discussed in the section that follows.

When evaluating their teaching, all three novice teachers said that if given the chance to teach the same level the following semester, they would teach it differently the next time. As T2 noted in one group discussion, she felt that one of her previous lessons was "dry" because of the book she was made to use: "It wasn't successful. It was very dry." She also stated that if she did teach it again, "I would like to teach it differently," though she acknowledged that it would take more work for her. T2 continued: "I'm finding this book is lacking a little bit of extra stuff but it would take me a little bit more work finding this stuff because I'm the one who has to go find it, but I just haven't had the time." She did not elaborate on specific additions she would make to her lessons, except to say that she would do more if she had a chance to teach the same level the following semester.

### Reflective Break

- Do you think it is natural for all teachers regardless of their experience to wonder if their students are bored during lessons?
- Do you worry about this and if so, how will you deal with it?
- If you don't worry about your students feeling bored during lessons, why not?

- All three novice teachers felt inexperienced and inadequate at times, and found that it was difficult to deal with students who needed special or extra attention in the classroom. How would you handle such students?
- T1 mentioned that lack of experience is not that important if one is excited about what one is doing and that one can overcome any mistakes. What do you think?
- Do you think that teaching style should always be matched to learning styles?
- Do you try to match your teaching style with your students' learning styles?
- How do you determine and understand your students' learning styles?
- T2 wanted to give her students more work in her lessons but was afraid that the students' might complain because she said she realized the school in which they teach "is also a business." What do you think about T2's ideas?
- When you finished your first semester teaching did you decide that if given the chance to teach the same class again you would teach it differently? If yes, why, and what changes would you make? If not, why not?

## Evaluating Learners

Another issue that was often discussed in the group meetings by all three novice teachers was that of attendance. This issue covered not only the question of whether learners actually came to classes, but also the fact that when they did come to class, some were constantly late or left early, some were rude, and this all negatively impacted the flow of the lessons. The issue of students' presence in class actually began in the first few weeks and some of this was beyond the control of the three novice teachers because some students started the program late and the administration continued to place new students in different levels well into the fifth week of the semester. All three novice teachers noted that this situation made life difficult for them in many ways, especially when they had to give marks to a student who had missed a significant amount of classes.

In terms of student placement in classes well after the semester had commenced, T3 said that she was given a new student five weeks into the program, and the student wondered if he would pass the course because he had started late. T3 reported that the student came up to her after his first class and said: "'Do you think I can pass?' And I said, 'Well, you've missed five weeks and we're halfway through, so this could go any way.'" Then T3 said that she really had to think about what to say to the student after that because it was a real and serious issue, and because she could not dismiss him. So she said that she broke down the skills that the student could concentrate on, such as Speaking, so that he could get good marks on these particular skills at least. T3 told the group: "So, I said, 'Maybe you should be very concerned with Speaking with your Writing and Grammar teachers because you probably could pass Speaking.' We'll see where it goes." Then T3 also noted: "Attendance is important we know, but they are not going to be held back just because they've missed their first two weeks." To which T1 added: "As long as they do well." However after this issue arose in the group discussions all three novice teachers realized that they really did not know what they should do or how they could find a solution to this beyond asking someone else at the school. They did not say if they in fact asked others in the school about this issue and it did not come up in any later group discussions beyond the mid-point of their first semester teaching.

In terms of students not attending classes, T1 noted that she had students who did not come to class and as a result also did not hand in assignments, which created problems for her when trying to figure out how to grade these students. T1 remarked: "I have some students who don't come to class and they're not handing in assignments, but that's the only mark I can judge them on. If they haven't handed them in, they don't get marks for it and that will affect their final grade." She continued: "I have one or two students that are scraping by and it's more because they don't come to class and they're not handing in assignments but that's the only mark I can give them as I can't give them marks if they don't come to class."

One reason that T1 gave for some of these students not coming to class was that because they had reached the highest level (Level 5) and they thought they could skip the classes because they would not or could not fail as they had already been given conditional admission to attend regular university classes. As T1 noted:

> I have a few that I feel like I have to track them down and say, "What's the problem? Why aren't you coming to class? You haven't handed in any book reviews, this is the fifth one. What's going on?" kind of thing. If it is just because they don't care, fine, I'll leave you be, but you are going to fail and will not be allowed to enter university.

T1 then talked about one of her students who she said she considered did not care about the lessons, because he did not hand in any homework he had been assigned in the first few weeks although she reminded him about this several times:

> I said, "You do realize that you haven't handed in any of the four book reviews up to now." Then he replied: "Oh, I'm going to hand them in." I said, "No, they are due every week. It's not something you're just supposed to hand in when you feel like it. So you realize you have zero for four book reports." He said "Oh, okay." So, I, I got the feeling after talking to him that he just doesn't care.

After this exchange T1 said that she decided not to ask him again as she felt his answers were dismissive and rude and that it was up to him from then on. She reflected: "That's fine. I'm not going to push him."

T2 agreed and went on to say that some students were not only late for class but also rude when in class. As a result she did not have time to focus on the content of her lessons because she had to spend extra time on these students, and this caused stress. T2 continued:

> I have a student who doesn't do his work. We're writing, and he is sitting there. I said, "When are you going to start writing?" and he replied "Oh, I'll do it later." Then I said, "This is an in-class assignment, okay." But he still just sits there.

T2 said that she felt frustrated because the student just stared at her and she did not know what to do about him. She remarked: "I feel really frustrated at such times because I am not sure what I can do, not to mention this student has already missed eleven days."

T3 agreed with the other two novice teachers about rude students and talked about one student who was always late for her classes and when he was in class, tended to be rude. T3 remarked: "That student shows up late, and I was explaining that next Tuesday you need to know your debate topic in your group. He says, 'You should be saying this Tuesday because today is Wednesday.'" T3 said that she was at first shocked and unsure about what to do with this student and his comments, but this time she said that she decided to confront him:

> I said to him, "Pardon me?" Then he says, "You should be saying this Tuesday because next Tuesday …. There is a big difference between this Tuesday and next Tuesday." Then I said, "As far as I'm concerned it's next week, right?"

T3 said that she was upset at his constant interruptions of her instructions as he tried to find anything that he could make fun of in a sarcastic way, not to mention his continual late coming to her classes.

## Reflective Break

- Do you think it is the teacher's responsibility to motivate all students to attend class regularly?
- Do you think it is the teacher's responsibility to motivate all students to be on time for each class?
- What would you do if a student did not come to class regularly?
- What would you do if a student was always late for class?
- What would you do if the administration kept adding students to your class weeks after the beginning of the semester?
- What would you do if a student did not hand in homework regularly?
- T3 decided to confront one student who regularly failed to hand in homework. What do you think of her actions?
- T1 decided not to "push" a student who despite reminders was not handing in a report. What do you think of her actions?
- Do you think that ESL teachers are under extra pressure to pass language students who have been given conditional acceptance (conditional upon successful completion of their English language program) to a university degree program, or do you think they can fail them if they do not attend or hand in assignments?
- What experiences if any have you had with having to pass ESL students just because they have been given conditional acceptance to a university degree program?

## Generating Solutions

Although the teachers realized that they could not solve many of the issues that arose during their first semester teaching, they attempted to generate their own solutions to as many issues as they could because they realized that they had to survive. One such issue that they were able to discuss in the group meetings, and as a result generate a rather innovative solution, was how to deal with dominant students in their classes. All three novice teachers had such students, and all of them said that they found it especially important to deal with these types of dominant students immediately; otherwise they said they feared they would lose control of the class.

This issue was first brought to the attention of the group by T2 when she relayed how she had some "domineering students," and was unsure what to do about them. During the group discussion that ensued, T1 suggested that T2 should "Tell him to come up and teach the class." T1 continued that for her it was a "good tactic that worked. They like to be the center of attention, but they don't like it if *you* put them at the center of attention, usually."

T3 then related how she sometimes used a technique called "Talking Sticks." She said that she would give each student two sticks that could be of different colors to indicate how much time the student would be allowed to speak. Each time they spoke in the class they had to hand in a stick, and when the two sticks were gone they could not speak anymore in that class. T2 said that she would try this in her class in the week that followed, to deal with the domineering students.

In the group meeting the following week T2 said that she had implemented the "Talking Sticks" approach where she gave "each student two sticks and when they had spoken, they had to give one stick to the teacher." T2 said that for one particularly dominant student this ensured that: "Once his sticks are gone, he has got to be quiet." She told all the dominant students: "Sorry, you lost your chance .... Next time you are going to be smarter with how you use your sticks."

Then T2 said that she had discovered something very interesting and surprising to her as a teacher. She found that using the "Talking Sticks" not only stopped some students from dominating the class discussions, but it also encouraged those she considered to be shy students to speak more in class. And when they did speak, T2 said that she was surprised at how good their English speaking ability was. This resulted in a more even distribution of student talking time in her class. T2 noted:

> My shy students realized that I care about them as well, and even if I cared before, now I can really show them that. It also showed my talkative students that the class is not only about them; that they have to share with others. I have noticed that my shy students actually are more concise and can express their points very well.

Not only did T2's students appreciate that she showed she cared but they also appreciated that she gave them an opportunity to practice their English. T2 said: "One student that said it gave them opportunity to speak. She said, 'It made me think faster because I knew I had to use my sticks; otherwise I would be stuck in class.'" The student told T2 that before the class using the Talking Sticks: "I was always too intimidated to speak, and I was trying to hide behind my fears, but you made me speak because I had to use my sticks. And I found this was a very good thing."

Another question that was often discussed by all three novice teachers was how to deal with students who were disrespectful, typically by being rude or off task in lessons. T2 noted that there were some students who masked rudeness and inappropriate behavior with trying to be friendly with the teacher. She said that she was very cautious about being too friendly with students and kept her communication with them within the school environment. As T2 said: "Being friendly with students has to be taken at a very, very cautious level otherwise you are going to get really taken advantage of." To which T3 added that some students had asked her to add them as friends on Facebook but she had refused: "I have students who said to put them on my Facebook. I said, 'No.'"

T1 said she tried to use humor when students were off task. When the whole class seemed to be off task, T1 said that she stopped everything and tried to bring them back together. She said that this could happen at the beginning of the week when she was trying to get them focused after the weekend, or at the end of the week when they were looking forward to the weekend. T1 noted that this happened in one of her writing classes and that she felt frustrated because all her students were staying off task. She described her response:

> So I just kind of said to them, "You know what guys. Come on. We need to be on the same page," because they were doing the writing and we were trying to get through the planning outline and get to the first draft, so I could give the feedback and whatever. It's frustrating for me.

She said that she warned them if they did not finish what she wanted them to complete, they would have to do it as homework. T1 continued: "Some people come up and say, 'Well, I don't have my topic planned yet.' So I said to them, I said, 'If you do not get it done in class, you have homework. That's all there is to it.'" T1 noted that the threat of homework seemed to be successful because when she asked who had completed the task at the end of the lesson, "They all came with their, their first draft done. So that was good. Hopefully that will continue." She also said that some of her students did not complete the task properly so she had to assign it for homework, but she also realized that she would have to give them some incentive to do the homework. She said: "I have to say that these are for homework marks and if you don't show up for class tomorrow with your homework, then you don't get the mark."

**Reflective Break**

- What would you do with domineering students in your class?
- What do you think of the Talking Sticks solution?
- Do you allow your students to add you on Facebook? Why, or why not?
- What do you think of the teacher using humor as a solution to some classroom problems?
- What do you think of the threat of giving extra homework as a solution to some classroom problems?

## Conclusion

This chapter has outlined and discussed how the novice teachers evaluated their lessons, their teaching and their learners and how they attempted to generate some solutions to the problems they encountered. They especially talked about their need to keep control of their lessons and how to deal with students who require special or extra attention in the classroom and those students who are disruptive, and come late. The group meetings helped to generate some solutions to these problems. Each novice teacher had her individual approach to the issues she faced, and in the course of the semester developed role identities of her own as a teacher, based on her personal beliefs, values and emotions. These role identities are discussed in the following chapter.

# Chapter 7

# "I Want to Be Me": Role Identity Development

## Introduction

Up to this point I have presented what the three novice teachers talked about in the group discussions, which included the experiences they considered important during their first semester as ESL teachers. During this first semester all three of them were developing as teachers, and in particular they were developing individual roles, or role identities, that are important to consider in terms of novice teacher development. Burns & Richards (2009: 5) have suggested that role identity "reflects how individuals see themselves and how they enact their *roles* [emphasis added] within different settings." Role identities, according to Cohen (2008: 82), are "powerful organizing structures because people get recognition, positive reinforcement from others, and other rewards when they accomplish roles successfully." Teacher role identity includes teacher beliefs, values and emotions as they relate to many aspects of teaching and being a teacher. In this chapter I will present how the novice teachers' role identities developed during this first semester.

## Professional Role Identity

Professional role identity formation usually begins in pre-service teacher education programs; however, evidence suggests that in many such pre-service programs its formation and development, as Franzak (2002: 259) has noted, are "best seen as a by-product of teacher education programs rather than a targeted outcome, at least from the student teacher's perspective." Then when they begin their careers in a real school setting, issues related to role identity resurface, but this time its development entails, as Achugar (2009: 65) has observed, "positioning oneself in relation to others by differentiating, affiliating, challenging, or accepting certain ways of constructing knowledge, being, and doing in the world." For many novice teachers this need to "be positioned" in terms of role identity can come as another shock (see previous chapters about other shocks) because the ideals that they may have built up in their initial teacher education courses may seem very distant when they are asked to take on roles that they may not have been prepared for during their courses.

Teacher role identity formation and development can occur on two different levels: when the language teacher receives formal training in a teacher education program for entry into the TESOL profession, and as the teacher conceptualizes his or her own identity during this process. One is external to the teacher-learner (i.e. the teacher education requirements) and the other internal (i.e. the teacher-learner's attitudes about his or her new career as an ESL teacher). Teacher-learners can also form and develop their professional role identities while they are being socialized into the profession during their first year(s) in the job. As Varghese, Morgan, Johnston & Johnson (2005: 37) have noted, the socialization process during the first year of teaching includes "a process of identification—that is, of acquiring an identity, of becoming someone or something." When ESL teachers enter the workplace for the first time after qualifying, they must negotiate contextual factors that, as Miller (2009: 175) has noted, are far from their experiences on "their pre-service education courses" and as such may be outside their control. The contextual factors ESL teachers in their first year(s) must negotiate include workplace conditions, curriculum policy, bilingual policy, cultural differences and social demographics of the students and the school. Negotiating these challenges, as Miller (2009: 175) has observed, "forms part of their dynamic of professional development."

Thus, as novice teachers are being challenged from the moment they enter the classroom in their first year, they inevitably encounter issues and events that make them reflect on the various roles they take on or are given at the time. Teacher role identity includes all the functional roles a teacher uses while performing his or her duties, what he or she feels and believes about teaching and being a teacher, and how these are shaped by his or her evolving teaching philosophy as a novice teacher (Walkington, 2005). For the purposes of this chapter, then, novice ESL teacher role identity indicates the configuration of interpretations that the teachers attach to themselves in terms of the different roles they enact (either voluntary or ascribed) and the different professional activities that they participate in, as well as how others view these particular roles and activities. In order to explore the three novice teachers' role identities, the transcripts were coded for both explicit and implicit references to professional role identity, where explicit references include statements a speaker makes that refer directly to a role identity such as "a teacher" and "when we teach," while in the case of implicit references speakers construct identity roles without stating or naming them directly. The identity roles were then tabulated for the number of occurrences, but those role claims that appeared infrequently (less than three occurrences and with only a passing comment) were not considered. What follows is a detailed discussion of the categories of professional role identities that emerged for the three novice ESL teachers.

## Teacher Roles

Thirteen professional role identities emerged from the group discussions and these were further placed in clusters under the three main identities: *Teacher as Manager*, *Teacher as "Acculturator"* and *Teacher as Professional*. Table 7.1 outlines the identities within each of these clusters and their frequency of reference.

Table 7.1: Role Identities of Novice ESL Teachers

| Category | Role |
| --- | --- |
| **Teacher as Manager** | • attempts to control classroom; |
| *Communication Controller (7)* | • attempts to control communication and interaction; |
| *Arbitrator (5)* | • offers feedback (positive and negative) in the classroom; |
| *Motivator (4)* | • motivates students to learn; keeps students on task; |
| *Presenter (3)* | • delivers information. |
| **Teacher as "Acculturator"** | • helps students to get accustomed to life outside class; |
| *Volunteer (8)* | • gives time outside class to organized activities; |
| *Friend (5)* | • befriends students (offering advice and support); |
| *Care Provider (4)* | • plays a role of care provider for students. |
| **Teacher as Professional** | • dedicated to work; |
| *Novice (7)* | • *new* to teaching; |
| *Follower (5)* | • follows expectations of the administration; |
| *Unique (5)* | • is unique (differs from other teachers). |

As Table 7.1 shows, a total of thirteen role identities were distinguished and divided into three main clusters: *Teacher as Manager*, *Teacher as "Acculturator"* and *Teacher as Professional*. *Teacher as Manager* included four sub-role identities, *Teacher as "Acculturator"* had three and *Teacher as Professional* also had three sub-role identities. The frequency count of the occurrences of each role is also included in brackets beside each descriptor. Of course, some of these role identities may overlap and could conceivably be applied in a different cluster. However, they were assigned a given position because the data suggested that they are the closest representations of these role identities.

**Reflective Break**

- What is your understanding of the three main clusters?
- What is your understanding of each role?
- Are you surprised by any definitions of any of the roles you see?
- How would you define each role?
- Which cluster would you identify with most and which would you identify with least?
- Which cluster is most surprising for you?
- Which role is most surprising for you?
- Can you add more clusters and roles that you consider appropriate for your context?
- Do you think ESL teachers have different roles than teachers of other subjects?

## Manager

Teacher as Manager, which had four sub-identities, represents the role of the teacher as the person attempting to control what happens within the classroom. The three more frequently mentioned sub-identities within the *Teacher as Manager* cluster were *Teacher as Communication Controller*, *Teacher as Arbitrator* and *Teacher as Motivator*.

## *Communication Controller*

*Teacher as Communication Controller* (seven occurrences) was identified as a role where the teacher maintains the desired classroom dynamics, such as the control of turn taking and communication patterns. This identity role also includes the teacher's responsibility for matching up students to work with each other. One particular example of this came in the seventh group meeting when T2 related an activity she was trying in one class on how to deal with dominant speakers (as was outlined in chapter 6). In summary, T2 decided to introduce her idea of "Talking Sticks" because she had domineering students and in this way she would be better able to control the communication flow in her classroom. As she noted: "Once his [the domineering student's] sticks are gone, he has got to be quiet." T2 said she planned to introduce a further detail: "What I am going to do is I am going to color code how much [time each stick allows the student], like 10-second stick,

30-second stick, 1-minute stick." At the following group meeting, she reported on the results. She mentioned that she "would purposefully not let them speak" after they had handed over the stick: "Then I said, 'Sorry. All done!' I would take their stick, and they went 'Oh.' I was like 'I know you have something to say,' but I would not let them continue."

## Arbitrator

*Teacher as Arbitrator* (five occurrences) was identified as a role where the teacher listens to various issues raised by students about their learning and conduct and then makes a decision about what to do. Sometimes the teacher is "tough" on the students and sometimes "nice." An example of this came up in the ninth meeting when the teachers were talking about marking exams and that they tended to struggle with being too easy or too hard on the students. Later, in another group meeting, they talked about how they had all gotten tougher on their students by giving their questions back to them. T2 gave an example:

> I asked them a question and I said, "What do you think?" and one student said to me [gave an answer] ... "Oh, is that correct?" I asked the student. And she says, "I don't know. You're the teacher." And I said, "Oh, but you are the student. You have to make a decision if you agree with it." She looked at me like, "Well, just tell me if I am right or wrong and be done with it," how to break that, I don't know.

T2 went on to say that even though "generally the students at first are shocked," and respond "Aren't you the teacher? Why are you asking us?" they would get used to it.

## Motivator

*Teacher as Motivator* (four occurrences) means the teacher wants to keep the class interactive and all the students interested. An example of this was when the teachers brought up a point about teaching paraphrasing and hinted that they would like more engagement from students while teaching this particular activity. They noted after some classes that they would like to teach differently the next time and next semester because they figured some classes had not gone so well, and then they suggested that the textbooks were a probable cause because they were boring.

**Reflective Break**

- What is your understanding of each of the roles outlined above?
- How would you rank the above roles in terms of importance for you and your context?

## "Acculturator"

*Teacher as "Acculturator"* represents the role of the teacher as one who does work or activities outside the classroom, helping students to become accustomed to the local culture. The three sub-identities within this cluster were of teacher as *Volunteer*, *Friend* and *Care Provider*.

## Volunteer

*Teacher as Volunteer* (eight occurrences) is a role identity where the teacher gives time outside the classroom to organized activities, although in this case the contract teachers were expected (one could say even required, although, according to the teachers, it was never actually put down on paper or expressed) to go on cultural outings with students in their own time. This volunteering was, according to the teachers, supposed to be helpful to ensure future contracts. One such example was a teacher volunteering to go on a pumpkin-carving trip with the students because "They asked for volunteers." Another said that she "might as well volunteer" for the trip considering the number of emails she received but, as she noted, "Sometimes I don't want to volunteer, and if you don't volunteer, what does that mean? That you're unpopular." Another teacher agreed and expressed the opinion that "You're signed up for outings. I was signed up to the pumpkin farm, okay. It was a forced volunteer. They forced me to volunteer."

## Friend

*Teacher as Friend* (five occurrences) is where the teachers say they make personal connections with their students. However, this was not always a role identity valued by the teachers. One teacher suggested that she was cautious when it came to making friends with her students, and did not agree when they suggested that she should add them on Facebook. The same teacher also noted a feeling of conflict with this identity role: "As much as I want to be part of their experience, I cannot because eventually I felt like students were not taking me seriously anymore. I was just a peer. I was not a teacher any more." Another teacher suggested that friendship must be balanced: "I go a little over and above with relationships with the students because I'm social and that's important. But, I don't want to feel taken advantage of and I don't want to ... I have to balance my own life, my family life."

## Care Provider

*Teacher as Care Provider* (four occurrences) suggests the identity of a teacher in a guardian role, one most likely linked to gender as all three teachers were female. An example of this role identity arose was when the teachers were talking about how they had to constantly remind their students to complete various forms, which made them feel like a mother to them. One teacher noted that "it took 20 to 25 minutes in one class doing all of the administrative stuff and it cut into 25 minutes of my lesson plan ... because some of them were sitting in class [saying], 'Well, I don't know my postal code.' I said, 'You're not taking these papers home. Leave them with me. Bring your postal code tomorrow.' 'Oh, I forgot it again today.' So, I guess that's where I guess I'm feeling like their mother."

### Reflective Break

- What is your understanding of each role above?
- How would you rank the above roles in terms of importance for you and your context?
- Do you think the term "acculturator" is unique to those who teach English to speakers of other languages? Why, or why not?
- Do you think ESL teachers must go beyond the classroom to help their students, such as volunteering, doing stuff as a friend outside class and so on?

## Professional

*Teacher as Professional* represents the role of the teacher as one dedicated to her or his work, and who takes it very seriously. An example of this arose when one teacher shared a story about the teaching methods of a colleague she was talking to one day and realized that she perceived a lack of professionalism on the part of the teacher in the encounter. The teacher noted that this colleague, a new teacher herself, never prepares for classes, and states that she herself needs to be prepared. She says: "I need to be prepared. I know myself. Teaching is my job and it should be done properly. I can't take the easy way out. It's not fair [to the students]." There were further sub-identities noted within Teacher as Professional, and the most frequently mentioned were *Teacher as Novice*, *Teacher as Follower* and *Teacher as Unique*. It is interesting to note that all these sub-identities, though they seem distinct, are in many ways intertwined.

## Novice

*Teacher as Novice* (seven occurrences) means the teacher has little to no experience, is new to teaching. This could include teachers anywhere, from those having just started out as teachers of ESL to those with just a few years' experience. As one can imagine, this was noted by the teachers in the early part of the semester with many explicit statements about how everything was new to them. The novelty changed a little as the teachers gained more confidence through the semester and began to recognize that, although they were still novices, they now had some built up experience and knowledge especially related to the students they had been teaching. However, this development was not always recognized by the people who made the decisions within the institution. For instance, T1 noted this towards the end of their first semester when collaborating with another novice teacher on making an exam. She commented on their being knowledgeable about their class and content taught but that their exam was not accepted, possibly because they were novice teachers.

Even though T1 disagreed with the decision, she decided not to fight it: "I thought, no. But instead of arguing the point we just got an exam that was 'approved' from another more experienced teacher who was teaching the same level, and used it." On reflection, T1 noted that she was "willing to take advice" because she was a novice teacher.

## Follower

*Teacher as Follower* (five occurrences) is related to the novice identity role outlined above and denotes a situation where the teacher is required to follow the expectations of the administration (e.g. teaching style, curriculum expectations and lesson plan submissions). However, they do not always do so exactly and even when they do, it is not always happily. An example of this arose when T2 was discussing how they were expected to follow the school's prescribed syllabus for teaching. T2 said that she was "given kind of a course outline, I have to follow" and then she noted that she was not afraid to go outside the syllabus if she thought it was useful for her students. As T2 noted: "I just have to realize that if there is something that I have to go away from the textbook for, in order to meet the essay expectations, I'll do that. If there is something that I can really use then I'll use it." T1 said that she found the requirement to collaborate, write and submit lesson plans to the institution "pointlessness." In addition, this teacher noted that if she followed what the institution required her classes would be boring. She continued:

> They expect me to teach pronunciation and they say "Here's the pronunciation book." And then they say "Make their class fun. Experience the language." It just kills me that I'm expected to do it. I'm like, every Friday I'm dreading because the students just sit there like this [mimicking a bored voice] "Tea, Tom, Door." Click the tape off. "Okay everybody get up. Take a deep breath. Stretch! Everybody's awake. Sit down." It is absolutely brutal.

## Unique

*Teacher as Unique* (five occurrences) is when the teacher has a stated unique teaching style which differs from everybody else's. This identity role emerged early in group meetings as the teachers were trying to figure out their role in the institution. For example, as was noted above, these teachers were required to collaborate and submit lesson plans; however, one of the teachers voiced some resistance to the idea of collaborating on developing and discussing lesson plans with other more experienced and established teachers in that institute because she regarded this process an impediment to her teaching style. She continued: "I want to be me. I want to submit my lesson plans detailed according to my style, not according to five other teachers who are collaborating. If my long-term lesson plan is approved, then leave me alone." She later continued on the theme of wanting to be different than the other teachers in the institution where she worked. She said: "I want to be an individual. I don't want to be just part of the faculty where everybody is getting the same. I want them [students] to come away with the same skills acquired, but I want to do it my style."

**Reflective Break**

- What is your understanding of each role above?
- How would you rank the above roles in terms of importance for you and your context?

## Ready-Made or Self-Constructed Roles?

Some roles are taken on and some roles are given to us by others. So a central question related to role identity that is pertinent to the above taxonomy outlined in Table 7.1 is whether these roles have been predetermined (given by others) or individually constructed (taken on either consciously or subconsciously) by the teachers. In other words, do they just fit into these roles by following preexisting patterns, or have these roles developed over time through their interactions with other teachers? The difference between these two positions (imposed roles as opposed to roles assumed by teachers) is really one of what can be perceived as being *ready-made* roles versus *individually created* roles that have been negotiated over time. No doubt some roles also fall in between, so we really talk about a continuum with ready-made roles at one end and individually created roles at the other.

Creating awareness of the existence of such identity role descriptors enables novice teachers not only to consider which roles they are involved with, but also who created these roles and if they want to continue with them or to create new ones in their stead. In other words, it is important for novice teachers to be able to articulate, not only to themselves, but also to their colleagues and administrators, which roles have been ascribed to them and which assumed by themselves, and if any of these roles conflict with their teaching or with the institution where they teach. For example, it could be suggested that the identity roles of teacher as unique, arbitrator, learner, motivator, presenter and care provider that emerged were individually created (either consciously or subconsciously), while the roles of teacher as follower, novice, friend, volunteer and communication controller were more predetermined and some possibly ascribed to the teachers by the institution or people within that institution.

Once roles have been identified, they can be reflected on and then the question can be asked if such roles are still relevant for the teacher after this articulation. For example, the cluster *Teacher as Professional* provides some interesting contrasts and indicates that these novice teachers may be struggling between their individually created role identities and those that may have been ascribed by the institution.

For instance, the identity role of *Teacher as Unique* as a descriptor for a novice ESL teacher could be seen as problematic not only by the institution, but also by more experienced colleagues within that institution who may think these novice teachers do not have enough teaching experience to be able to fulfill such a role.

In fact, *Teacher as Unique* conflicts with other roles, such as *Teacher as Novice* or *Teacher as Follower*, which also emerged from the group discussions but were more predetermined by the institution and context. It seems that these novice teachers were struggling with the required role of having to follow procedures already established in the institution where they worked, while at the same time trying to maintain their individuality as teachers. Yet, they readily admitted to being novice teachers with a lot to learn, and expressed willingness to act in a collaborative manner with their colleagues.

The novice teachers in this group also seemed to be struggling with the cluster *Teacher as "Acculturator"* where roles such as *Teacher as Volunteer* were taken on by the teachers sometimes willingly but sometimes because they felt it was expected of them. Of course, because they were in a part-time capacity in the institution, they also felt that not to take on such roles as care provider and social worker or indeed to appear unfriendly (the opposite of *Teacher as Friend*) towards students would impact their chances of being rehired for another four-month contract (each year consisted of three such contracts). Indeed, *Teacher as "Acculturator"*, whether voluntary or mandatory, seems to be a professional role unique to the ESL teaching profession and as such should be directly addressed in language teacher education courses so that novice ESL teachers are ready for such a unique role, rather than being surprised by it, as was the case with the subjects of this study.

## Reflective Break

- Why is the concept of "self" important to consider when reflecting on a novice teacher's role?
- Why do you think novice teachers do not generally consciously reflect on the roles they are given or the roles they take on?
- How does reflecting on a novice teacher's role reveal the complexity of a language teacher's work?
- How do the various roles outlined in this chapter indicate the complexity of language teaching?
- Do you reflect on your various roles as a novice teacher?
- If yes, what are these roles, and if not, why not?
- Which of these roles did you choose?

- Which of these roles were you "given" by the institution and/or your colleagues?
- Do you think your school/institution imposes any roles on you as a novice teacher?
- If you have roles imposed on you by the institution, which of them do you think are not in your interests?
- Why do you think the role "teacher as acculturator" brings ESL teachers in closer proximity to their students than would normally be the case for teachers of other subjects?

## Preparing Novice Teachers for Roles

Novice teachers may not be as well prepared (as the three novice teachers in this study attested to) for the different identity roles they take on or are allocated in their first year(s) of teaching. In fact, Miller (2009: 174) has pointed out that within TESOL there seems to be a "serious hiatus between language teacher education courses and the lived experiences of teachers." Consequently, Miller maintains that there needs to be a shift in language education to "critical sociocultural reflection, which takes account of identity and related issues of individuals in specific contexts, and of the role of discourse in shaping experience" (ibid.: 178). For example, teacher-learners, while still on pre-service courses, can be asked to reflect in an anticipatory manner on these three umbrella identity clusters and what they mean for them. They can also be asked to consider other roles that they may have to take on in the future once they have graduated and how their identity will change from pre-service teacher to newly qualified ESL teacher. Chapter 9 outlines how novice teachers can be better prepared in their teacher education programs for the role realities they will encounter in their first year of teaching.

## Conclusion

This chapter has outlined and discussed the thirteen different novice teacher identity roles that emerged from the group discussions. When novice teachers consciously reflect on the various roles they take on or are given to them by their institutions, colleagues or others, they can start the process of trying to figure out who they are and who they want to become as they continue their teaching careers. These roles will inevitably change over the course of their careers but as novice teachers they are still being formed. As T2 noted: "I think I will be forming my role as a teacher forever. I mean, no matter how much you're formed you still have to somewhat alter it to your class because of the class dynamics of each class is different." An exploration of these role identities also allows language educators a useful lens into the *who* of novice teachers and how they construct and reconstruct their views of their roles as ESL teachers in relation to colleagues, administration and context. This knowledge can be fed back into language teacher education programs in order to prepare learner teachers more effectively for the reality of the different contexts in which they will be teaching. This will also be of help to them in developing their own individual styles of teaching, as will be discussed in the next chapter.

# Chapter 8

# "You Put Your Personal Stamp on It": Reflecting on Teaching Style

## Introduction

We all remember the teachers we loved most at school, as well as the teachers we did not like so much; but most of all, we really remember the teachers who seemed different than all the others. These memories of our "special" teachers are centered on their teaching style in the classroom; in fact, they have put their personal stamp on their lessons. Teaching styles, a topic I briefly introduced in chapter 6, represent a teacher's behaviors that appear in how they conduct their classes. Some of these teachers may have been teacher-centered in approach, some more learner-centered, and some more content-centered. As Saracho (2000: 300) has pointed out, a teacher's teaching style reflects the "the specifics of their preparation, their instructional situation" and how "individual teachers respond to their students in their own unique way." This chapter explores the notion of teaching style as a subconsciously held assumption, as reflected in how each of the three novice ESL teachers responded to their practice in their own ways and what the sources of their beliefs about teaching and learning were.

### Reflective Break

- Can you remember the teacher that left the most positive impression on you in (a) grade school and (b) university?
- Why did that teacher leave such a positive impression on you?
- What activities and methods did this teacher use?
- Can you remember the teacher that left the most negative impression on you in (a) grade school and (b) university?
- Why did that teacher leave such a negative impression on you?
- What activities and methods did this teacher use?

> - What is your understanding of teaching style?
> - Do you have a particular teaching style? Can you describe it and then explain where it originated from?

## Factors That Influence Teaching Style

Teaching style is a difficult concept to define and as someone once said it is not unlike the six blind men trying to define an elephant: each held different parts of the elephant in his hands and as a result gave different descriptions of the elephant. For example, the person holding the trunk said it was like a snake; the person holding the tail compared it to a rope; the person holding the leg compared it to a tree. So too, trying to define teaching style can lead to different emphases because at any given moment in a classroom a teacher's style represents a complex array of mental and physical acts. However, there is agreement that in general terms teaching styles represent "those enduring personal qualities and behaviours that appear in how we conduct our classes" (Grasha, 1996: 44). Thus, teaching style is an important concept because, like role identity, it often reflects a teacher's values, beliefs and emotions, which have a bearing on how a teacher acts during the teaching and learning process in a classroom.

However, it is not easy to clearly identify a teacher's natural teaching style from just observations alone given the vast number of factors that impact how a teacher actually delivers his or her lessons. Therefore, in order to capture a picture of the three novice teachers' teaching styles I examined all the comments of all three over the prolonged period of the group meetings as the closest proxy to their classroom practices. Key findings from this close examination revealed that the main influences (in order of frequency) on their teaching styles was their *personality* followed by their experience of *what works best,* their teaching *approaches* and *established practice*—all of which will be discussed in this chapter.

## Personality

The main influence by far (44 per cent of total comments) on teaching style, as revealed in the group discussions and various classroom observations, was teacher personality. Just as presumed by Bailey et al. (1996) and Richards & Lockhart (1994), language teachers may have a personal preference for a particular teaching style because it complements their teaching personality, and all three teachers in this group show a similar influence of their personality on their teaching styles. Teacher personality for the purposes of our study included any reference to a specific characteristic, a preference, an interest or a unique way of doing something as a teacher. For instance, T1 noted that she wanted to follow her own way as a teacher when she said: "We were educated to engage our students, so I'm not always comfortable following a template for my teaching." T1 continued that her personality as a teacher is most important for her because as she said: "My teaching style is different. You have to put your personal stamp on it."

T1 recounted that her way of teaching is similar to her personality in that she does not want to force students beyond a gentle push to do anything they are not interested in. T1 wondered if this was the "mother" inside her, and said:

> I don't think it is so much mothering, but, I don't know. How do you know that these students just don't want to put any effort in or how do you know that maybe they need just a little push because they're not quite getting it or they just need someone to show concern, right? I don't want to babysit them. They're adults. I understand that.

T1 then recounted how she noticed that one of her students seemed to show that he did not care but she was determined not to take any marks off him just because of his attitude. T1 instead decided that she would show the student that she was concerned about him and see if this would work, as this was what she would be comfortable with. T1 noted: "Some do not even care but I will show how concerned I am with this one guy, I have the feeling that it's just that he doesn't care, and that's fine." T1 added that she has always tried to show her concern for her students and that she does not hold them to assignment due dates if they do not hand them in on time: "I've never said to a student: 'This is the due date and tomorrow I am no longer accepting it.' I don't care. Maybe someone else will take 10 per cent off. I wouldn't take it off." T1 also stated that if her students are late, she does not come down too hard on them:

> I've been pretty lenient. If they had only just not been doing this all the time, I would still have cared about the one or two minutes being late because I know they don't have a lot of time between classes.

During this conversation about T1 allowing students to hand in assignments when the students are ready, T3 noted that it was not in her personality to be able to do this. T3 said that she was tougher on students and if the students did not want to work, then she would not make them. She noted that this was her "way," and continued: "I'm getting a little tougher because they, they can give you any excuse out of the book." T3 reflected: "When things don't work out, I'll just give it up. Forget it. Let's do something different." T3 also remarked that her teaching style is heavily influenced by her personality: "Teaching is a personality issue for me because there comes a point when for my own mental health ... I have to follow what I think is correct."

T2, as well, mentioned that her teaching style is a reflection of her personality. She noted that she is a planner and her personality makes her want to plan everything well in advance: "I plan everything in my head. I'm a heavy planner. I'm not a procrastinator." T2 added that she does this whether inside or outside the classroom but that for teaching she prefers to have deadlines to follow and wants her students to also follow the deadlines she sets for them, unlike T1 above. T2 remarked: "I'm better on a deadline. When I have a date to put the marks in, I have put my students' marks on there. So, they actually know their actual marks on time."

## Reflective Break

- Do you think your personality influences how you teach? If yes, how? If not, why not?
- Are you aware of your students' learning styles? If so, how do you suit your teaching personality to their styles?
- Do you take on a "teacher persona" that may be different than your real personality?
- What did T1 mean when she said: "I'm not always comfortable following a template for my teaching"?
- T1 said: "You have to put your personal stamp on it." Can ESL teachers be "themselves" while teaching? Are you?
- All three novice teachers seemed to have different beliefs about what to do with students who do not want to work hard. What are your beliefs about this issue?

## What Works Best

"What works best" refers to any practice that the three novice teachers perceived as being successful in their work as an influence on their teaching style. One example discussed in the group meetings was T1's confidence in developing a particular lesson plan by herself: she did not share it with the other teachers of that level, and did the activity she had planned in her class without telling anyone how it worked. T1 said, "Well, I'm just going ahead with my own plan anyways and just do it on my own." After the lesson she said that she was happy because it worked well and that she would use it again in other classes. T1 remarked: "I think that you just have to try not to over-use it like every activity, but I think it's a good idea, and it worked very well." T1 noted that she decided not to tell anyone because she knew that what worked best for her may not work for them and she did not want to have to explain what she had done to the other teachers. She said that her teaching style would be influenced by what worked best for her as this made her life as a teacher easier.

T3 also relayed that she is influenced by what works best for her and for her this concerns always trying to follow routine in her lessons. She said that she likes to follow routine and that she thinks her students too like to follow routine; she feels that it works better with beginning students. T3 said: "I think routine is very good. My class [a beginning level class] is working on paragraphs and they should know what is required and what works for writing." For teaching writing, T2 noted that she would take anybody's suggestion if she thought it would work.

All three novice teachers communicated their opinion that the books they are given to teach each skill do not work for them and that they have to use their own materials that they know work much better. For example, T1 noted that when teaching pronunciation, "It's hard to teach when you have a tape that is not perfect and you don't have good sound." T2 said: "Sometimes I take my textbook and throw it over my back and say, 'I know. It's boring for me too.' I say, 'How do you think I feel? You just have to look at it one semester but I get to see it for years on end.'"

## Reflective Break

- Do you have activities and methods that work best for you when teaching ESL?
- Are these the same as your favorite activities?
- How do you determine if a method "works" in your class?
- Do you think that students' reactions are always a good indication of their learning?
- What if you are using activities that have always worked best in your classes before but involve hard work from your students, and they react negatively to this practice? Would you change your practice or would you insist on using it because it has worked well in the past?

- Do you think that teachers can get stuck on their beliefs about what has worked best in the past and ignore their current students' reactions that may necessitate changing a particular practice to suit their learning?
- Do you think teachers should follow routine when teaching?
- What would you do if you were given a textbook that you considered was boring to use?
- What would you do if your students thought the textbook you were using was boring but you thought it was good for your students?

## Teaching Approach

Teaching approach refers to an approach (or method) that the teacher has used or is going to use in their lessons because they are comfortable with this approach. A typical example of a favored approach was revealed in a group discussion that was centered on methods for assessment of students. T3, for example, noted that one of her classes on pronunciation required students to give a speech. When her students gave the speech as part of their assessment, she would video-record it and then do a type of simulated review with each student after the class where they would go over the speech by watching and listening to the tape. Then she would comment on how they did with their pronunciation. T3 said: "When making assessments, I reviewed all of mine because I video-taped all of their speeches and then reviewed them, and then I offered them the opportunity to come in the office and go over them with me, so we can work on their pronunciation ... I wrote notes, all the pronunciation problems."

T1 discussed how she teaches her writing classes using her own approach that is different than the textbook because she said she finds the textbook limiting. T1 reflected on this class: "I can use my stuff [approach]. I'm finding this book is lacking a little bit of extra stuff, like extra paragraphs to read or extra materials to make the concept I am teaching clear." For example, T1 relayed how she needs to follow her own approach to teaching writing because the book does not do a good job in explaining paraphrasing. She then explained her approach:

> I asked them, "What is a paraphrase?" Because I didn't want to just read it right out of a book or whatever. So I kept asking them for, for things they could tell me about paraphrasing. So I would just write things on the board as they came up with the ideas. I let them, and not the book, come up with the ideas.

Regarding their general approach to teaching, all three novice teachers said that they would like to teach the same skills to the same levels the following semester so that they could improve on their teaching methods. T2 remarked: "I was thinking I would like to teach the same things next semester to make it better." To which T1 replied: "Then you can always go back into your old lesson plans and revise." T2 then remarked she would have liked to have gone over her lessons this semester to see how she could improve her teaching approach and methods but that she had no time as things were moving too fast for her, so she noted it was a good idea to teach the same classes the following semester because she could compare her teaching methods: "I would like to look at them [lessons] in more detail to see if I can see some patterns, but I haven't had the time. I hope that I can learn something from it and if I have the chance to do this class again and make some changes in it."

### Reflective Break

- What are your favorite approaches to teaching the four language skills of reading, writing, speaking and listening?
- Have you ever experienced any resistance to any particular approach you tried when teaching any of the four language skills?
- Do you try to "sell" your particular approach to teaching the various skills if your students resist?
- Have you ever modified your approach to suit your students? If so, do you consider this the same as modifying your beliefs or do you still keep the same beliefs about a particular approach?
- If you modify your approach yet keep the same beliefs as before, do you think your classes are real for you as a teacher?
- Do you think that all three novice teachers can benefit from teaching the same classes (skills) to different students the following semester? Why, or why not?
- Do you think they can improve their teaching methods by teaching the same classes (skills) or by teaching different classes (skills)?

## Established Practice

The fourth (in terms of frequency count) biggest influence on teaching style was established practice. This was basically any statement that referred to an established way of doing something in the school. However, all three noted that even though they were influenced by established practice it was a reluctant influence and they only followed it because they had to as novice teachers in their first semester. Indeed, all three novice teachers noted early in their first semester that there were certain established ways of doing particular things within the school that they would have to follow, such as having to deliver lesson plans to lesson coordinators each week, but that they did not like this. T1 noted: "I'm just doing it [writing lesson plans] because I need to do it because somebody told me I need to do it. There is really no value in doing lesson plans."

In addition, they were indirectly informed that they were supposed to collaborate if possible with others teaching the same level when making those lesson plans. T1 said: "They wanted us to each do one week of lesson planning, and we did our long-term plan. I don't mind collaborating for the purpose of expressing ideas." However, T1 said that she did not like this established practice in the school because she said that it did not help her teach: "You have to do every lesson plan in order to be confident in the classroom for your own self, so I don't see the value of collaborating, like taking someone else's lesson plan and there I go. That doesn't help." So T1 said that she pretended to collaborate with the other teachers of her level when doing the lesson plans but once in the classroom she followed her own approach, as noted above, because she said that she could not teach to another person's lesson plan.

T3 noted that she was trying to collaborate with another teacher teaching the same level and they came up with a way of dividing the work when completing lesson plans. T3 said: "I was splitting the weeks with the other teacher, but what I do is I go over, I ask her to send it to me via email. I do my own changes and then, it's fine with me."

T2 said that she too tried to follow this established way of collaboratively preparing lesson plans, but in contrast to the other two novice teachers, this collaboration seemed to be working for her. She said: "I'm doing that [collaborating] with a teacher who is teaching the same level and skill because I have two sections and she has one, but we're working well together with the lesson plans."

## Reflective Break

- What are the established practices in your school?
- Do you think teachers should follow the established practices in the school they are teaching in even if these conflict with their beliefs?
- How far would you go to follow an established practice of the school if it was in conflict with your approach to teaching English?

## Conclusion

From the group discussions and interviews outlined in this chapter, it seems that all three novice teachers' personalities have a direct influence on how they perceive they carry out their classroom practices. Given that teaching style involves the implementation of that teacher's philosophy about teaching, it is important then for teachers to not only to become aware of their teaching styles but also what influences these so that they can reflect on their relevance for their current practice. Indeed, an important question for the TESOL educators is to what extent a teacher shapes his or her teaching approach to suit his or her personality. As such, all (novice and experienced) ESL teachers should reflect on whose needs they are fulfilling when they are teaching: their own by choosing approaches that suit their personality only, or their students' learning needs, and styles. Perhaps a happy medium is to try to attend to both sets of needs, as all three novice teachers attempted as reported in this chapter. However, in order to be able to achieve such balance novice teachers will need to be given opportunities to reflect on the sources of their teaching styles and their impact on instructional decisions. In such a way, teachers will be able to make more informed decisions about the approaches they choose and consider whether these approaches are still providing optimum opportunities for their students to learn. For this to happen, novice teachers will need to become reflective practitioners and this process must begin in teacher education programs. The next chapter discusses how novice teachers can be prepared in teacher education programs to be reflective practitioners throughout their careers, but especially in their first year of teaching.

# Chapter 9

# "Remember All You Learned at ___": Reflective Practice within Teacher Education

## Introduction

In the first chapter I talked about the transition from trainee to novice and how novice teachers must endure a shock when they make such a transition. Novice teachers experience such a shock mostly because they are not prepared well for what they will face in real classrooms and real schools. One of the reasons given for this state of unpreparedness is that the TESOL profession does not have many examples or accounts of what novice ESL teachers actually experience in their first year of work (see chapter 2). Consequently, this book has outlined some of the issues that arose from an in-depth study of a group of three novice ESL teachers in Canada (see chapter 2 for details on the group) in order to be able shed some light on these important experiences (see chapters 3 to 6). In addition, in chapter 2, I talked about some novice teachers' experiences of being told that their teacher education courses had been a waste of time and that they should "forget all you learned at ___" (fill in the blank with the name of the teacher education program).

In this chapter I return to the transition from teacher education program to the first year of teaching, or from trainee to novice, but with a different message learned from the experiences of the three novice ESL teachers reported on in this book. If we examine the headings of many of the chapters— *The First Week Is Like You're in a Swamp," "Here's the Book, Go Teach," "It Was Very Dry," "I Want to Be Me," "You Put Your Personal Stamp on It"*—we can see that the findings reveal that the three novice teachers experienced "praxis shock" or the challenge of coping with classroom realities for which their pre-service training had not adequately prepared them—as borne out in the title of chapter 2: *"Forget All You Learned at ___."* In this chapter I outline what teacher education programs can do to help make the transition less of a shock and more reassuring by preparing the trainees to deal with some of these real experiences. Hence the title of this chapter is: *"Remember All You Learned at ___ "* (fill in the blank with the name of the teacher education program).

> **Reflective Break**
>
> - What is your understanding of "Remember all you learned at ___"?
> - What do you remember from your teacher education program?
> - What is the role of a teacher education program?

## Mitigating the Praxis Shock

Learning to teach ESL is a complex process because the learning does not only take place during the first year of teaching; other influences have an impact on how novice teachers are socialized into the profession, such as the influence of their schooling, and the influence of the teacher education program they graduated from. Most second language teacher education programs consist of foundation courses which are usually followed by some form of teaching practice.

Although not all programs offer the same background training for pre-service teachers, most trainees become familiar with a range of different teaching skills through these courses and develop a solid knowledge base derived from their academic studies during that time. In addition, most pre-service teachers experience some form of teaching practice in order to develop their teacher knowledge and teaching skills. The activities provided through teaching practice—which typically include planning lessons, teaching different parts of a lesson, observing and reviewing teaching—usually provide pre-service teachers with an overall understanding of teaching ESL. However, there is evidence in general education research literature, and now from the experiences of the three novice ESL teachers reported on in this book, that these programs do not adequately prepare teachers for the realities of their first year of teaching. For example, all three novice teachers reported that they experienced a "praxis shock" as they were challenged on how to cope in a new professional world that they felt they were not very well prepared for.

The goal of language teacher education programs is to educate novice teachers so that they can enter the TESOL profession. However, if novice ESL teachers are left to struggle in their first year (as reported in this book), then there is a good chance that some may get so frustrated with the praxis shock they encounter that they leave the profession. Thus one main goal of all pre-service language teacher education programs (regardless of the specific content of these programs) should be to try to mitigate this transition/praxis shock in whatever way possible so that experienced teachers will not say "forget all you learned at ___" but rather they will be able to advise novice teachers to "remember all you learned at ___" because they know that the novice teachers have been prepared adequately to be able to meet the various challenges they will inevitably encounter in their first years. One way language teacher education programs can help mitigate the transition/praxis shock is to guide pre-service teachers in the reflective practice process throughout their *teacher education* program (as discussed in this chapter) and encourage them to continue this reflection in their *first year* (covered in chapter 10).

### Reflective Break

- How do you think novice teachers should be prepared to mitigate the transition/praxis shock that many experience during their first year?
- What role should teacher education programs play in this preparation?
- Why should novice teachers be encouraged to continue to reflect on what they have learned in their teacher education program during their first year?

## Teaching in the First Year

Because teaching experiences are so varied, unpredictable and thus contextualized, language teacher educators must prepare pre-service teachers for the unknown. The best way they can do this is to increase their awareness through reflective practice. Novice teachers need to be prepared for the reality of what they are about to face and this can be achieved through reflective practice instruction to help mitigate any problems that occur. Through reflective practice, novice teachers can also fill in any gaps that may appear in any mentorship program (if indeed any mentor has been appointed). However, this reflective practice should not be just a cursory discussion but an all-out course that is devoted to providing pre-service teachers with the tools of reflection so that they can be better prepared for the transition from the teacher education course to the first year of teaching. As mentioned in chapter 1, to do this it is necessary to add a supplementary course that specifically addresses the needs of novice teachers, called "Teaching in the first year" (see Farrell, 2009).

**Reflective Break**

- Did you have any course like "Teaching in the first year" in your teacher education program, which helped you prepare for the reality of teaching in your novice year?
- If yes, explain what you did in it.
- If not, would you like to have had such a course and what would you like to see covered in such a course?

## Developing Skills in Reflective Practice

"Teaching in the first year" can provide opportunities for pre-service teachers to develop skills in reflective practice so that they can better manage the various issues, challenges, conflicts and problems they may face in their first years of teaching. This reflective approach to language teacher education supports Wright's (2010: 273) observations that language teacher preparation should place "an emphasis on the student teacher's learning to teach, and becoming a thinking teacher" which "in turn means a great deal of reflective activity programmed into learning experiences."

However, pre-service teachers should not be just asked to be reflective without receiving support in how to become so. Such support structures are provided in a new framework I recently developed that promotes reflection at five different stages/levels: *Philosophy*; *Principles*; *Theory*; *Practice* and *Beyond Practice* (Farrell, 2015a). Although each of the five stages/levels within the framework are treated separately below, readers should realize these are not isolated but are all linked; each stage or level builds on the others and all stages must be considered together to give us a holistic reflective practice experience. Each stage/level can be explored on its own in order to allow teachers to focus on specific aspects of their practice at a particular time.

## Philosophy

*Philosophy*, the first stage/level of the framework, can be considered to be a window to the heart of a novice teacher's practice because having a philosophy of practice means each observable behavior has a reason that guides it even if the teacher does not articulate this reason. In order to be able to reflect on our basic philosophy we need to obtain self-knowledge and we can access this by exploring, examining and reflecting on our background from where we have evolved. This includes our heritage, ethnicity, religion, socioeconomic background, family and personal values that have combined to influence who we are as language teachers. An exploration of teacher life-histories can provide deep insights into the roots of teacher practice and identify the very seeds of the philosophy of practice. For example, each pre-service teacher can be asked to consider who it was from their past that influenced them to become an ESL teacher.

For example, when T1 reflected on her life-history she noted that in elementary school she had a teacher who "made sure I understood the difference between grammar points I was having trouble with." In other words, she noted that she wanted to be like him as a teacher because he "encouraged me in my school work even though I was not a very academic student and pushed me." T1 maintained that this attention made her "feel special and helped me think that I could do well in school." As a result, T1 said that she would try to be a similar type of teacher as this elementary school teacher. In addition she also noted that she had a French teacher who took the opportunity to talk to her students inside and outside of class. T1 noted: "She was excited to teach the language and that showed in her teaching. She made opportunities for us to use the language by arranging an exchange trip to use the language." Thus, T1 said that she too would give her students opportunities to use English in real-life situations whenever possible (her observed classes throughout the first semester seemed to reflect this philosophy), and would take every opportunity to talk to her students also outside of class.

When T2 reflected on her life-history she noted a specific instance from her Grade 1 class that reminded her why ever after she said she had wanted to be a teacher: "I knew that I wanted to be a teacher when I was in Grade 1." T2 then recounted the story of the day she heard her teacher asking a student a question about colors and she said: "I knew that that student was colorblind, I also knew that he was very shy and embarrassed about it." That day T2 said she told the teacher about the student's colorblindness. As she recounted: "I advocated on his behalf that day, and I have been doing it ever since." So T2 stated that as a teacher she will advocate for her students because: "I vowed that day that I would always try to understand my students." She acted on this throughout the first semester of the group's existence.

In contrast to the others, T3 remarked while reflecting on her life-history that she never considered she would be a teacher when she was growing up; instead she said she "stumbled upon teaching [ESL] really by accident." Herself a speaker of English as a second language, T3 said that she had become more interested in teaching when she moved to Canada, so she decided to get her ESL teaching qualification. It was during this qualification program, she said, that she realized that this would be her life's work: "Once I stepped into a classroom, I knew that this is exactly what I wanted to do for the rest of my life." However, she said that she had one serious issue to overcome as a teacher, and that was the difference between what was expected from a teacher in her home country where the teacher is viewed as a holder of all knowledge who will transfer that knowledge to students, and in Canada where she noted that her "first TESL teacher came to classroom and said that he does not have all the knowledge and has no problem telling his students if he does not know something." Her conception of the teacher as all-knowledgeable was still evident in classroom observations when T3 attempted to answer the questions of students from countries she considered had a similar view of the teacher; however, when she was with students who had a North American or European type view of the teacher as someone who may not have all the answers, she seemed to be more relaxed in dealing with their questions (see the critical incident report below for more on this).

In a similar manner, as part of their teacher education program pre-service teachers could be asked to tell their stories of who they are and what kind of teachers in the past may have influenced them, and then reflect on how they may still influence them (for good of for bad) today.

## Reflective Break

- According to Bullough (1997: 19), telling one's story "is a way of getting a handle on what we believe, on models, metaphors and images that underpin action and enable meaning making, on our theories." Write your autobiographical sketch that outlines some of the realities, dilemmas, joys and rewards, and your hopes for your future teaching life.

## Principles

*Principles*, the second stage/level of the framework for reflecting on practice, include teachers' assumptions, beliefs and conceptions about teaching and learning. Teachers' practices and their instructional decisions are often formulated and implemented (for the most part subconsciously) on the basis of these underlying principles because they are the driving force (along with philosophy reflected on at level/stage one) behind many of their classroom actions. It is important for teachers to articulate their underlying assumptions, beliefs and conceptions about teaching and learning because eliciting such details can "provide a meaningful basis for discussion and reflection" (Basturkmen, 2012: 291).

The driving force in terms of assumptions and beliefs behind the three novice ESL teachers' practices as reported in this book was their personality, as outlined in the previous chapter. This was followed by their experience of what works best, teaching approaches and established practices. All three teachers had strong personalities that were manifested through their style of teaching. T2 said that she had already realized that she has a strong personality that is difficult to change regardless of her teaching experiences. She noted that although she recognizes that she may need to change her teaching style depending on who she is teaching, she will not change it a lot: "I know I still have to somewhat alter it … because the class dynamics of each class is different but not that you are going to change yourself permanently or 100 per cent to a different person." T2 said she tells her students that she is who she is, and believes this is the correct way for her to teach, so she will not change. She remarked: "I tell my students upfront that I will not change," and "I have my principles" (see chapter 8 for more details on this topic).

## Reflective Break

In terms of being able to access our underlying assumptions, beliefs and conceptions about teaching and learning, Richards & Lockhart (1994: 6) have pointed out that this "involves posing questions about how and why things are the way they are, what value systems they represent, what alternatives might be available, and what the limitations are of doing things one way as opposed to another." Try to answer the following questions (adapted from Richards & Lockhart, 1994) about your teaching beliefs and classroom practices:
- What are my beliefs about teaching and learning?
- How do these beliefs influence my teaching?
- Where do my beliefs come from?
- What way do I actually teach in the classroom and how do I know what I do?
- What do my learners believe about learning?
- What do my learners believe about my teaching?
- How do these beliefs influence their approach to learning?
- What learning strategies do my learners adopt?
- What learning styles do my learners favor?
- What is my role as a language teacher?
- How does this role contribute to my teaching style?
- What do my learners perceive is my role as teacher?

## Theory

*Theory*, the next stage of the framework for reflecting on practice, explores and examines the different choices teachers make about particular skills taught (or that should be taught)—in other words, how to put what they have learnt into practice. Influenced by their reflections on their philosophy, and their principles, teachers can now actively begin to construct their theory of practice. Teachers reflecting on theory at this stage/level consider the type of lessons they want to deliver on a yearly, monthly or daily basis. All language teachers have theories, both "official" theories they learn in teacher education courses and "unofficial" theories they gain with teaching experience. However not all teachers may be fully aware of these theories, and especially of their "unofficial" theories that are sometimes called "theories-in-use."

Reflection at this stage/level in the framework includes considering all aspects of a teacher's planning (e.g., forward, central and backward planning) and the different activities and methods teachers choose (or may want to choose) as they attempt to put theory into practice. As they reflect on their approaches and methods at this level teachers will also reflect on the specific teaching techniques they choose to use (or may want to choose) in their lessons, and whether these are (or should be) consistent with the approaches and methods they have chosen or will choose. In order to reflect on these they will need to describe specific classroom techniques, activities and routines that they are using or intend to use when carrying out their lessons. Chapter 5 has provided details of what the three novice ESL teachers discussed in terms of their approaches and methods during their group meetings, and this took up over 60 per cent of all the group comments. Thus, theory in this sense seems to be important for ESL novice language teachers and as such they should be encouraged to consciously reflect on their approaches and methods in teacher education courses as outlined in chapter 5.

Another means of reflecting on theory is to explore and examine *critical incidents*. Although critical incidents are situations that actually occur during practice (the next stage/level in the framework), I include them now because they can be used to guide a teacher's theory-building. A critical incident is any unplanned or unanticipated event that occurs during a classroom lesson, and is "vividly remembered" (Brookfield, 1990: 84). However incidents only really become critical when they are subjected to conscious reflection. When we reflect on critical incidents, we can begin to understand the theory behind practice. Critical incidents can be written up as case studies as well, so another means of assessing theory reflections is to explore and examine different case studies of specific events that have occurred in teachers' practices. However, both are slightly different: whereas a critical incident is a retrospective analysis of any unexpected incident, a case study starts with the identification of an issue and then the selection of procedures for reflecting on it. It is important to reflect on both critical incidents and case studies because, as Shulman (1992: xiv) has pointed out, both provide "teachers with opportunities to analyze situations and make judgments in the messy world of practice, where principles often appear to conflict with one another and no simple solution is possible."

A critical incident poses a particular anomaly for a teacher, between what he or she conceptualizes as practice and an actual classroom experience that may run counter to such a conceptualization. In addition, critical incidents may also arise when a classroom experience runs counter to past teaching decisions, and this can cause teachers to perceive dissonance between their beliefs and theories and actual practice. Many teacher education programs do not prepare novice teachers to be able to recognize and deal with such teaching dilemmas, but these do originate in practice and as such need to be documented and reflected on.

T3 related one such incident that later reminded her of her life-history reflections outlined above. One day, she said, she suddenly had a new student show up five weeks into the term. In addition, on arrival the new student did not look happy and did not want to interact with female students from different countries, but would not explain why. T3 noted: "I gave them all an activity to work on in groups, but he just sat there by himself, with an attitude." Then she said that she did not know if "he was happy to be put down a level in the middle of semester to her class." T3 said that this new student did not want to work in any group and just sat there. What was also worrying for her at that time was that he tried to "influence another male student from the same country, who had been fine up to this, to join him." T3 said that she was trying to give her students more freedom to do what they wanted but this was a sudden challenge for her so she did not do anything at that time. She allowed her class to continue with the groups talking and people walking around as they wished, as this was the system she said she had wanted to develop.

However, she continued to think about the incident for some time after. As she said: "I have to say that I it really bothered me at first." So she tried to figure out why it bothered her. T3 noted that she understood that her students "come from countries where teachers most often have control of everything that goes on in a classroom [and] he probably was shocked to find his class in some form of chaos." In fact, she stated, she herself comes from an educational background where the teacher has total control of the class all the time:

> I came from the same structure and perhaps was trying a bit too hard
> to break away from total control. As during my first classes I give more

freedom to the students so they can get comfortable talking to each other I should have explained the purpose to my students. To them the whole situation looked like I have lost the control of the classroom.

T3 said that she realized that she too may not be fully comfortable in allowing group work with students wandering about her classroom, given her own background. She realized that she might have to adjust her use of group work as a result of this incident. T3 continued:

> I've decided to keep a closer eye on the teacher/students interactions and control vs working chaos in the class. So far today I felt like it worked better and a more controlled (not totalitarian) atmosphere helped shy students find their voice and express themselves. I will still use group work but not 90 per cent of the time.

When asked about the overall result of her reflecting on this critical incident, T3 said: "I think I learned that I next time I will ease my students into North American style of learning/teaching slowly and explain (a bit) the value of the effort that they have to put into working in what seems like chaos."

It is clear therefore that second language teacher education preparation programs should provide teacher learners with opportunities to practice reflection on critical incidents. I have highlighted some issues pre-service teachers can reflect on with the inclusion of a supplementary course that specifically explores and examines the first years of teaching. Such a course is also designed to support, as Johnson (2009: 10) has noted, "the development of teachers' adaptive expertise." Thus, during the transition from training to teaching, novice teachers, as Richards (1998: 164) points out, must be able to construct and reconstruct "new knowledge and theory through participating in specific social contexts and engaging in particular types of activities and processes." Indeed, I hope experienced ESL teachers will be able to say to all their novice teachers in the future: "*Remember all you learned in the course* when you are teaching in the first year."

## Reflective Break

- What is your understanding of T3's critical incident?
- How is this critical incident linked to her life-history sketch?
- Do you have any similar experiences?
- How can analyzing critical incidents lead to a greater awareness in teaching?

- Have you ever experienced a critical incident during class? If so, describe the incident and explain why it was critical to you.
- Report (in writing or orally) on a recent critical incident in your teaching using Thiel's (1999) four steps:
  1. Self-observation—identify the significant events that occurred in the classroom.
  2. Detailed description of what happened—describe the incident itself, what led up to it and what followed.
  3. Self-awareness—analyze why the incident happened.
  4. Self-evaluation—consider how the incident led to a change in your understanding of teaching.

## Practice

Up to now, the framework for reflection has emphasized philosophy, principles and theory, or the "hidden" aspect of teaching. We may think of the whole teaching process as an iceberg, where we cannot see the part that is beneath the surface of the water (the "hidden" aspect), which is much larger than the visible part on the top. All we can see is the top of the iceberg, or 10 per cent of the whole. In teaching this constitutes our *practice*, the fourth stage/level of reflection in our framework. Thus we are now ready to reflect on the more visible aspects of what we do as teachers, our *practice*, and what actually happens in the classroom. Reflecting on practice begins with an examination of our observable actions while we are teaching, as well as our students' reactions (or non-reactions) during our lessons. Of course such reflections are directly related to and influenced by our reflections on our *theory* at the previous level (e.g., see critical incidents above) and on our *principles* and *philosophy*.

At this stage/level in the framework, teachers can reflect *while* they are teaching a lesson (reflection-*in*-action), *after* they teach a lesson (reflection-*on*-action) or *before* they teach a lesson (reflection-*for*-action). When teachers engage in reflection-in-action they attempt to consciously stand back while they are teaching as they monitor and adjust to various circumstances that are happening during the lesson. This includes reflecting on how the students are responding or not responding, how long each activity may be taking and/or how individual students are interacting with the content of the lesson. When teachers engage in reflection-on-action they are examining what happened in a lesson after it has taken place and this is a more delayed type of reflection than the former. When teachers engage in reflection-for-action they are attempting to reflect before anything has taken place, to anticipate what may happen and try to prepare for this before they conduct the lesson. Ideally the results from the first two types of reflection (reflection-*in*-action and reflection-*on*-action) can be used as a basis for future planning (reflection-*for*-action), and this as such is slightly different than the type of planning that was discussed in the previous stage/level of the framework.

Teachers have several different methods of accessing their reflections on *practice*. For example, they can engage in classroom observations (self-monitoring, peer critical friendships or group observations), and they can record (audio and/ or video) their lessons and later transcribe the recordings for a more accurate review of what occurred. However, one of the most common ways of reflecting on classroom teaching is to engage in classroom observations. Cogan (1973: 134) has defined classroom observations as "those operations by which individuals make careful, systematic scrutiny of the events and interactions occurring during classroom instruction. The term also applies to the records made of these events and interactions." These can be carried out either alone, with the use of a recorder (audio/video), and/or having a peer or facilitator observe classes. As was outlined in chapter 6, an interesting example of the power of classroom observations carried out with a peer or facilitator (in this case it was the facilitator) occurred in the middle of the semester in T2's observed class.

T2 invited me to observe her teach a series of her conversation classes with the general idea of providing her with "some" feedback on her teaching but without any specific instructions on what to observe. When she informed me about the time and place for the first observation and some details about the class such as the proficiency level of the students, the focus of the lesson and the instructional materials she would be using, we set up a pre-observation meeting to decide what the observation focus would be and what my role would be during the observation. After this pre-observation "discussion" we both agreed that the observer (this author) would use a seating chart observation record, or SCORE instrument (Acheson & Gall, 1987), to plot the communication flow during the class, if such an opportunity arose; otherwise he would take notes as well as make use of a video recording of the class.

The classroom observation commenced and after some initial instructions and a review of previous homework, the teacher started a question-and-answer segment with the class that lasted for 20 minutes, in which I coded using the SCORE chart. After this session, T2 broke the class into pairs and each pair was given a specific task to complete. The class ended in this manner, with student pairs given a homework assignment for the following class. Figure 9.1 presents the SCORE analysis of the 20-minute question-and-answer segment.

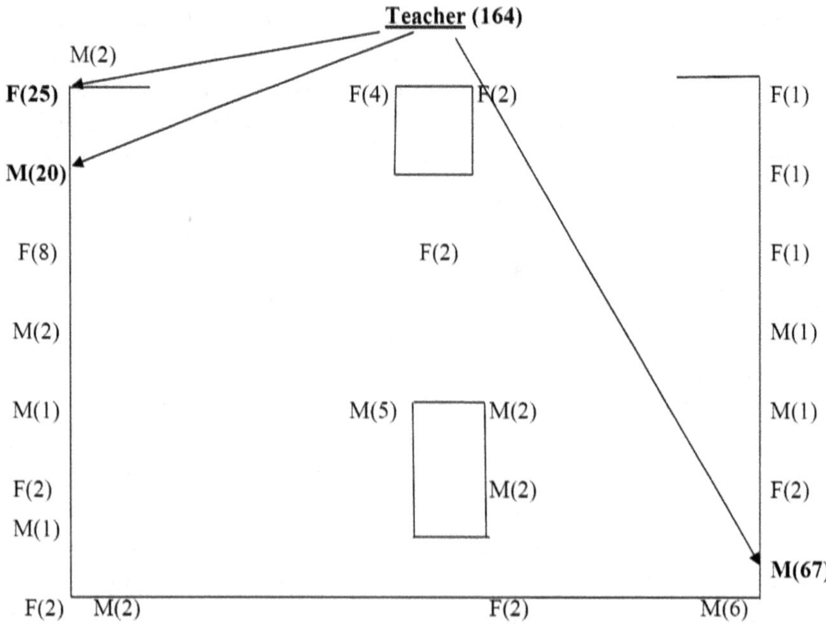


**Figure 9.1**: SCORE I

*Note:* F = female students (12); M = male students (13). The long arrows show the directional flow of the questions and answers between the teacher and the students who participated the most.

After the class we examined the SCORE chart for the 20-minute class segment that was focused on teacher and student interactions through questions. The students are all sitting in a large rectangle-shaped class with long outer tables and two inner tables. In a 20-minute period of interactions in T2's speaking class, for example, she asked a total of 194 questions. I divided these into the 164 questions she put to the 21 individual students (she noted that she intended to ask each student at least one question to make sure all spoke) and the 30 questions she put to the group, which works out at about eight teacher questions for each minute during that 20-minute period. T2 said that before class she had intended to ask each student at least one question during class to make sure all spoke at some time at least (the SCORE chart in figure 9.1 above indicates this). However, she said she was surprised to learn that she had such a high frequency of asking questions in total and per minute.

We also looked at the flow of the communication in terms of which students had participated the most during this segment. Before she saw the SCORE chart, T2 said that in her estimation everyone had contributed to the discussion and in general the rate of participation was equal among students. However, when we looked at the SCORE chart in figure 9.1, we saw that this class segment seems to have been dominated by one particular student, a male student in the bottom right-hand corner of the chart—M(67)—this means that he asked 67 questions. This number of questions accounts for 34 per cent of the total interactions during that segment. We also noted that two other students in the top right-hand corner of the class, one female student F(25)—i.e. , she asked 25 questions—and a male student who asked 20 questions, M(20), were also very active in this class segment, each accounting for about 12 per cent of the interaction time. T2 reacted with surprise to these findings as she had intended for this question-and-answer period within her speaking class to draw more or less equal responses from all students. The intention was that all students would be active and answer at least one question (the SCORE indicates she was successful here) but that no single student would dominate the question-and-answer period (she did not achieve this). T2 noted that she was aware that the student (M67) was relatively more active but had not realized just how dominant he was; and she was not aware at all that the two students in the top right-hand corner of the classroom were so active. So these two opposite sides of the room were very active, the bottom right corner and the top left corner (as highlighted in figure 9.1), but the rest of the classroom was comparatively quiet. For the following week T2 said that she wanted to expand the interaction within her classroom so that she could include all the students as equally as possible and especially not have any students dominate the class.

## Follow-Up

The following week during the group discussion, as noted in chapter 6, another teacher (T3) came up with the idea of using a method known as "Talking Sticks" to try to spread the frequency of communication in her class. T3 explained the "Talking Sticks" as follows: the teacher gives each student two sticks and tells them that they can only speak when they give a stick to the teacher, and must stop speaking when they have no sticks left. So T2 invited me to observe her class the following week in which she said she would try the "Talking Sticks" idea that was discussed in the group. I also conducted a SCORE analysis of this segment of her class as outlined in figure 9.2.

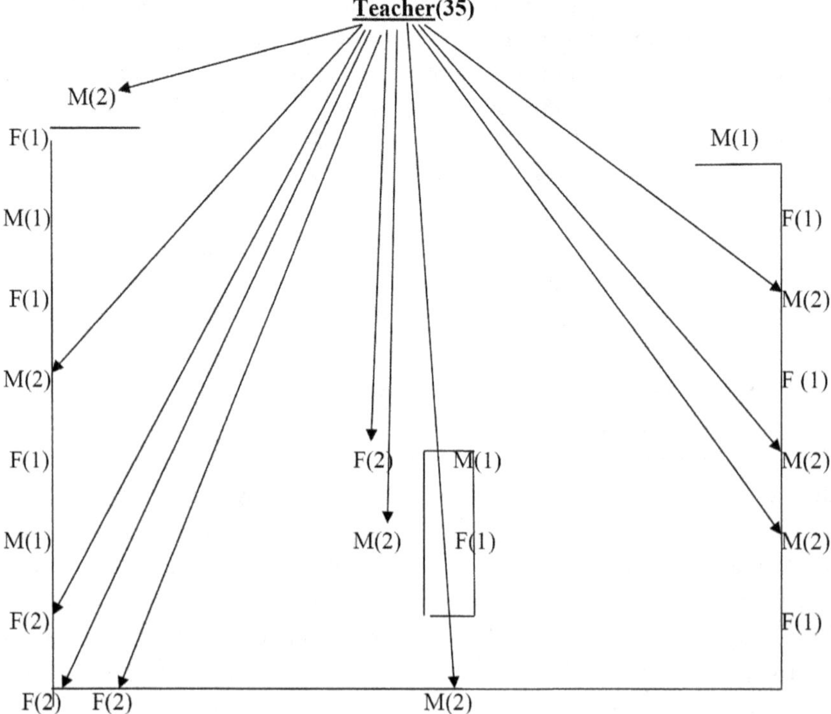


**Figure 9.2:** SCORE II

*Note:* F = female students (11); M = male students (11). The long arrows show the directional flow of the questions and answers between the teacher and the students who participated more than once. Not all questions asked by the teacher were answered.

The same students (of whom three were absent) were sitting in a large rectangular-shaped class with long outer tables and one inner table, somewhat similar to the previous class. We noted that in the 20-minute question-and-answer period the teacher asked a total of 35 questions to the class, with students being allowed to use the sticks for a maximum two turns to speak. This was much less than the 194 questions she asked in the previous class. We also noted that in a change from the previous class, many of the students took much longer for each interaction with the teacher and they also initiated two or three further interchanges as a strategy for lengthening their turn before giving their second stick to the teacher. As T2 noted when her "most talkative student" [M(67) in the previous class] wanted to speak more, she would not allow him to do so:

I asked him for a stick. He said that he doesn't have one. I told him that he cannot answer the question. He replied that he has a great point and a wonderful idea. But everyone [all the other students] told him that it doesn't matter since he used all his sticks. He had to be quiet. At the end of the class he told me that next time he will be very wise in how he uses his sticks.

## Reflective Break

- What is your understanding of the "Talking Sticks" idea that was first explained in chapter 6 and now in more detail using the SCORE chart to outline the communication flows before and after the use of the sticks?
- Have you ever tried to chart the communication flows in your classroom? If so, how did you do this?
- Find a critical friend and observe a series of each other's lessons and do a SCORE analysis to chart the communication flow in each class, then comment on whatever patterns you notice.

## Beyond Practice

The final stage/level of the framework entails teachers reflecting *beyond practice*. This fifth stage/level adds a sociocultural dimension to teaching and learning which, Johnson (2009: 2) points out, is "not simply a matter of enculturation or even appropriation of existing sociocultural resources and practices, but the reconstruction and transformation of those resources and practices in ways that are responsive to both individual and local needs." This is called *critical reflection* and entails exploring and examining the moral, political and social issues that impact a teacher's practice both inside and outside the classroom. Critical reflection moves the teacher *beyond practice* and links practice more closely to the broader sociopolitical, as well as affective/moral issues that impact practice. Such a critical focus on reflections also requires teachers to examine the moral aspect of practice—that is, the moral values and judgments that impact practice.

One of the criticisms of reflective practice is that it has been too individualistic in its focus given that teachers seldom work alone in a school or institution. In fact, most teachers must collaborate with other teachers in one way or another for many aspects of their teaching lives—coordinating, consulting, cooperating and/or communicating with each other even to carry out the simplest of acts in a school or institution. We are engaged in some form of dialogue with other teachers all the time and so we can move this one step further and try to engage in critical dialogue with them as well. Such critical dialogue about practice with other teachers is important and even necessary because as Crow & Smith (2005: 493) point out, "the process of engaging in a critical dialogue about one's practice is important not only in opening up one's reflections to public scrutiny but also, we would argue, in providing an ideal forum for collaborative learning." Such critical dialogue can be assessed by teachers talking in novice teacher reflection groups. Chapter 10 covers reflection beyond the classroom in more detail, as I outline how novice ESL teachers can collaborate during their first year of teaching in reflection groups and thus become more empowered as teachers.

## Reflective Break

- How critical should novice ESL teachers become when teaching in their first year?
- Do you ever consider whose interests are being served by your teaching English as a second language at the school or institution where you work?

## Conclusion

This chapter has outlined and discussed how novice ESL teachers can be better prepared for the praxis/transition shock in their teacher education programs and their first year of teaching (the latter is discussed in further detail in chapter 10) through instruction in reflective practice. However, novice teachers should not just be encouraged to reflect without receiving sufficient support in how to engage in systematic and structured reflection. The chapter thus presented a *framework for reflecting on practice* for second language novice teachers that has five stages or levels of reflection: *philosophy of practice, principles of practice, theory of practice, practice* and *beyond practice*. This overall framework is designed so that language novice teachers can bring to the level of awareness that which usually remains hidden—the interconnectedness of their philosophy, principles, theories, and practice and also their reflections beyond practice.

# Chapter 10

# "I Liked Hearing Other Ideas": Reflective Practice during the First Year

## Introduction

The previous chapter outlined and discussed how reflective practice can be the focus of a specific additional course, "Teaching in the first year," that all teacher education programs should adopt. This course can be called anything, really, as long as its core aim is to teach novice teachers how to systematically and consciously reflect on their practice using a particular framework such as the one outlined in chapter 9, adapted from Farrell (2015a). In this manner, novice teachers will be prepared to continue their reflections during their first year of teaching regardless of the context or school they find themselves teaching in.

Up to this point in their training and development, we can say that most novice ESL teachers have been consumers of others' knowledge rather than generators of their own knowledge. However, now that they have entered real classrooms they can begin to (re-)consider that knowledge and what they can apply to their particular context. So, as novice teachers obtain more teaching experience in their first year they will be able to generate their own knowledge as they begin to further consider their philosophy, beliefs, theories, principles. They can draw from these experiences and begin to theorize from practice, a crucial step for novice teacher development, as they make sense of their teaching during their first year (Richards & Farrell, 2011). In this way, Richards & Farrell (2011) maintain, novice teachers can develop an understanding of the underlying meaning of their practice and begin to formulate principles when planning and evaluating their teaching, with reference also to the personal philosophy which guides their decision-making. Thus the first year of teaching can provide the basis for novice teachers to begin to theorize from practice by articulating and then testing their philosophy, beliefs, theories and principles as they learn to teach in real classrooms.

This chapter suggests that if novice teachers have been adequately trained (e.g., with the addition of a supplemental course as outlined in the previous chapter) in the ways of reflective practice during their teacher education programs, they can use this training to become more proactive decision-makers during their first year. They can do this by taking more control of their experiences in this initial year by collaborating with other novice teachers in a reflection group. This novice teacher reflection group can be part of an official induction program or it can be independent of any induction program. Indeed, when schools do not have any induction program (as was the case for the three novice ESL teachers reported on in this book), these groups become especially important because they provide novice teachers a forum to talk about their experiences and problem-solve in a supportive environment.

## Navigating the First Year

Most novice teachers who have graduated from their teacher education programs and begun their first year of teaching do so with great enthusiasm, as was the case for the three novice ESL teachers reported on in this book. However, as we have seen in many other fields of education, many of these novices do not make it beyond the first year, which is usually the result of a general frustration with the reality of what they experience, such as poor overall working conditions that include long preparation and teaching hours, issues with classroom management including bad student behavior/lack of student interest, and difficulties in interacting with new colleagues, to name a few (Ingersoll, 2001).

In the field of general education the research on teacher attrition suggests that the inclusion of induction programs and mentors seems to help lower attrition rates (Huling, Resta & Yeargain, 2012; Ingersoll & Smith, 2004). Although the specifics of the implementation of induction programs will vary from school to school, district to district and country to country, overall it seems that at a mini-mum induction programs should be for at least one year, and should include some sort of reduction in teaching load, the allocation of a mentor and some other forms of teacher development opportunities for novice teachers during their first year (Huling et al., 2012). The main idea is that novice teachers are still learning to teach in their first year and they need support and feedback to be able to continue to build up their teaching confidence so that they do not become overwhelmed.

However, what happens if the school has no induction program and no men-tors appointed, as was the case for the three novice ESL teachers reported on in this book? In fact, as outlined in chapter 4, they reported that they were "just thrown in" without any kind of orientation and/or induction process. The school had an informal system of level coordinators and the three novice teachers noted that they "could" go to them for advice and help but that they always "seemed busy" and when they did help, it was hastily done and not of much use. In addition, the three novice teachers were expected to bear the same teaching workload as the experienced teachers, and when they first arrived were simply given the book and told to go teach the class (see chapter 4 for more details). There were no staff meetings that first semester and no assistance available for any of the three novice teachers. No collaborations were encouraged either.

In defense of the school I should point out that all three novice ESL teachers were under temporary contracts (as is the case for all novice teachers in that school when they are first hired) and as such the school administrators may have been reluctant to invest any time, energy or resources into guiding those they may have considered as transient teachers. Indeed it seems that in recent times in the Canadian context (and many other contexts worldwide) the majority of graduating ESL teachers have to take up in their first years such temporary, fixed-term contracts or some kind of relief-teaching with intermittent periods of no teaching if student numbers are low.

Unfortunately, this also suggests an informal entry into the profession that may constrain novice teachers' full development of their teaching routines, their relationships with students and colleagues, and even their mode of interaction with administrators. On the other hand, the only way all three novice teachers could ever hope to obtain a continuing contract is by taking on as many temporary fixed-term contracts as they can manage. Besides, they must take on volunteering duties whether they wish to or not, in addition to unreasonable workloads. Further, if they are to ever hope to gain permanency, they have to avoid complaining about anything, to make sure they are not seen as teachers who will be difficult as future colleagues.

What seems clear from various research reports (and from the results of the study in this book) is that, regardless of the type of employment contract, the notion that novice teachers should "sink or swim" is still deeply embedded in the teaching profession (see chapter 1 for more on the profession that eats its young). So what can be done to help novice teachers *swim* rather than *sink*, beyond the introduction of an induction program which seems painfully obvious but is ultimately the responsibility of the school/institution in which the novice teacher is appointed? One way of helping novice ESL teachers better navigate their first year of teaching is by engaging them in reflective practice in a *novice teacher reflection group* similar to the one reported on here.

**Reflective Break**

- What type of teaching contract do you have or did you have in your first year?
- If you had a short-term fixed contract, do you think this inhibited your development in any way?
- How do you get a full-time teaching contract in your context?
- What is your understanding of the statement: "the notion novice teachers should 'sink or swim' is still deeply embedded in the teaching profession"?

## Novice Teacher Reflection Groups: A Community of Practice

Because novice teachers are often left to sink or swim, as noted already in many chapters of this book, they tend to feel and become isolated thus further compounding whatever challenges they face because they have nobody (perceived or otherwise) to go to for help. The isolation does nothing to help them navigate these difficult waters because they cannot or do not reach out to others for advice and help, so unfortunately many do sink. As Shanker (1990: 210) has stated, it is: "the narrowness of the teacher's world which denies the possibility of satisfying exchanges with other adults in the sense that one is part of a thoughtful community of professionals."

This could have been the situation for all three novice ESL teachers reported on here, had they not been participants in the novice ESL teacher reflection group that was set up during their first semester of teaching. All indications are that the three novice ESL teachers used the group meetings to break from their isolation because they had no other forum in which they could really seek advice during their first semester. Thus, based on the results of the case study of the three novice ESL teachers reported on in this book, I maintain that other novice ESL teachers can also help themselves in their first year by forming similar reflection groups so that they can become more empowered from the very beginning of their teaching careers.

In the previous chapter I talked about reflection beyond the classroom and that this involves, among other things, reflection with others through dialogue and critical discussion. As Jay & Johnson (2002: 76) point out: "Reflection is a process, both individual and collaborative, involving experience and uncertainty. It is comprised of identifying questions and key elements of a matter that has emerged as significant, then taking one's thoughts into dialogue with oneself and with others." So in a general sense, a teacher reflection group is a community of practice in which members interact with one another as a means of "developing particular shared practices, routines, rituals, artifacts, symbols, conventions, stories, and histories" (Wenger, 1998: 6). More specifically, a teacher reflection group can be defined as "any form of co-operative and ongoing arrangement between two or more teachers to work together on their own personal and professional development" (Head & Taylor, 1997: 91). A novice teacher reflective practice group refers to a process in which novice teachers are provided a way to regularly and systematically reflect on their practice in a supportive, collegial environment that is usually free from evaluation. Such reflection groups involve novice teachers, as Humaira & Rarieya (2008: 270) point out, "undertaking an inquiry into their practice through verbally sharing, discussing, questioning and reasoning about their teaching experiences, either with their peers and/or a reflective coach."

## Process

As noted in the opening chapters of this book, the three novice ESL teachers set up a reflection group in part because they felt the need to talk about their experiences as each member was feeling lost during their first week. It worked out well for me as I was interested in hearing about the experiences of novice ESL teachers. We were put in touch with each other through a mutual friend, and I acted as group facilitator throughout the process. All three novice teachers were able to use the group as a sounding board when they shared many of their experiences in what turned out to be a supportive and collegial environment that was free from evaluation.

The novice ESL teacher reflection group followed the process that was described in chapter 2: we created opportunities for reflection, we negotiated particular ground rules, we made provisions for time, and we attempted to build trust throughout the process. At every meeting, each member shared issues and incidents that were critical to their practice. These issues were discussed and members attempted to come to some understanding of their relevance to their overall practices. They also attempted to reveal their teaching beliefs and compare these to their teaching practices so that they could take more responsibility for their actions, especially as these related to particular critical incidents. In addition, issues that were discussed in previous meetings were revisited for updated reports by individual teachers where appropriate. Each group meeting (which usually lasted one hour) followed the general format outlined below:

- The facilitator (this author) asked each member of the group what had happened of interest since the previous meeting. This could be a classroom problem, a critical incident or anything else of significance and interest for the teacher that had occurred during that week.
- After outlining the issue of interest the group then took up discussion of it, asked questions or sought clarification, and gave their opinions if warranted.
- The facilitator asked the teachers whose issues had been discussed in previous meetings if they had any follow-up to report. Or if the teachers had attempted to implement any particular changes in their teaching or in interactions with their colleagues or the school administration, they were asked for updates on these.

Even though we tried to follow the format above, the group had a somewhat open way of communicating these issues and incidents and I think this worked well rather than requiring members to relate or embellish incidents on a weekly basis. Instead, the group facilitator began each meeting with a general question such as: "Does anyone have anything of note that happened the previous week to talk about in the group?" In this way each group member could decide individually if they wanted to talk or not. They were not required to make anything up if they decided nothing of note had happened from their perspective.

The group talked about many different issues that involved them becoming more aware of their isolation as novice teachers, in that they knew that it was up to them to swim or sink because the school did not provide any particular induction program with mentor teachers to help them in their first year. The issues and challenges related to teaching that emerged in their discussions—such as classroom management, discipline and control, how to organize their lessons to motivate reluctant learners, student assessment, coping with materials they perceived as inappropriate or inadequate—seem to be universal for novice teachers as these same problems have come up in research studies in general education studies (e.g., Veenman, 1984). In addition, they also had to traverse their changing role identity as it developed during their first year.

One issue that the three novice teachers did not comment on was theory as it relates to professional knowledge, or the professional—practitioner knowledge divide. When they did come up with solutions to problems it was for other teachers' problems rather than their own. Perhaps this is a natural progression in problem-solving for novice teachers in reflective practice groups. Hiebert, Gallimore & Stigler (2002) suggest that the theory—practice chasm is similar to the divide between professional knowledge and practitioner knowledge. Professional knowledge, they note, is: "public, storable, and sharable, and serves as a mechanism for verification and improvement in teaching." However, they suggest that a practitioner's knowledge is linked to practice: "detailed, concrete, specific and integrated" (Hiebert et al., 2002: 24; see this source for more on this divide). Britzman (1991) notes the "dramatic shift" for novice teachers as they move from the teacher education program to teaching in real classrooms, and the disconnect between theory and practice formed because novice teachers were not given adequate support for thinking about their practice and how theory is an interpretation of knowledge about teaching, as well as considering their role identity shift from student to teacher. Britzman (1991) has suggested that theory and reflection help refine professional knowledge. Consequently, novice teachers should be encouraged to come together in teacher reflection groups during their first year in order to reflect on the relationship between theory and practice as they learn to think constructively about their practice. In other words, we can empower novice teachers through reflective practice in such groups.

**Reflective Break**

- The text above suggests that the following issues and challenges related to teaching that emerged in the discussions reported on in this book are universal. Give your opinion of each and add more of your own:
  - classroom management;
  - discipline and control;
  - how to organize lessons;
  - how to motivate reluctant learners;
  - student assessment;
  - coping with inappropriate or inadequate materials.
- Why do you think these novice teachers found it easier to solve their colleagues' problems rather than their own?

## Benefits

As the results reported in this book suggest, based on comments the three novice teachers made themselves, reflection in a group seemed to help them navigate this particular and complex stage of their career as novice ESL teachers. As the results have corroborated, novice teachers' first year of teaching can quickly become a battle for survival, as they become swamped and overwhelmed by the complexity of the changing identity roles they choose or are given, as well as by the demands and expectations of the school setting (students, colleagues and administrators). As Bullough (1997) has noted, teaching is already a demanding and stressful job but for novice teachers it can be even more demanding and really overwhelming if they do not have some help with the transition. This help can come from collaboration with other novice teachers in a reflection group.

As the weeks passed, the three novice ESL teachers began to get an overall sense of their professional efficacy, in that they felt that they were able to impact student learning, and their language about teaching and learning become more positive and hopeful towards the end of the period of reflection. The teacher reflection group played an important role in helping them reach this stage of hope because they were able to deconstruct various aspects of their first-year practices during the group discussions. As they began the weekly process of deconstructing, analyzing and making interpretations in the group with the aid of a facilitator, their sense of self-efficacy was increasing as they generated ideas about how to better control their professional world. The collaborative nature of the group enabled them to share critical incidents so that they could analyze and interpret them together and ultimately generate their own solutions, as the "Talking Sticks" solution testifies. Such group discussions need to be open and evaluation-free where each participant is willing to share their experiences, if they are to increase teacher efficacy. As Belmonte (2006: 117) has reported, "teachers who rely upon a network of other teachers have the best chance of soldiering on in the profession."

All three novice teachers stated that they found the group meeting very helpful. For example, T1 said: "I found it useful to meet just to bounce ideas off of, like because they're in the same position, so we could bounce ideas. I felt like actually we're reflecting on the teaching. I go home and I'm nice and happy. I don't have to complain to my husband about no meetings and all that stuff."

T2 noted that meeting in a group and talking about issues allowed her to hear her colleagues' ideas and get feedback from them:

> I liked hearing other ideas. I liked just getting some feedback when I said, "Oh, this isn't working in my class." Just to know that sometimes we were going through the same thing like, you know we were frustrated with the administration. We were frustrated with sometimes the students or whatever. So I think that's kind of nice because we created an opportunity to talk about ... you don't always have that opportunity in your office with a group of teachers.

T3 remarked that it was difficult for her to talk to other teachers because they always seemed busy when she wanted some information: "I did talk to other teachers [outside this group] but it's not set up that you're always free to talk and some of them are too busy marking." This is a problem because as Feiman-Nemser (2003: 29) has observed, "Without easy access to one another, teachers may feel reluctant to share problems or ask for help, believing that good teachers figure things out on their own." What usually occurs in many schools, as T3 noted above, is that experienced teachers tend not to want to interfere with novice teachers with the idea that they are too busy anyway, and so they do not share their experiences with the novices. Experienced teachers have survived their first years as novice teachers and perhaps they have come to their own terms with the isolation that many teachers feel in the profession; however, this isolation really damages a teacher's sense of belonging to the profession. As Brandt (2005: 21) notes: "Teacher isolation is a salient problem for all teachers, but the lack of collegiate interaction is especially relevant to novice teachers." Thus, it is important for novice teachers to have conversations with others during their first year and a reflection group set up within a school seems to be the best way to go about this. The question then becomes: What happens when all the group members are from the same institution?

As for having all three teachers from the same institution reflect together in one group, T1 noted that this was an advantage: "It actually worked out really well having all three people from the same, from the same program." In addition, because they are from the same institution they noted that they have become closer as a result of meeting regularly; this would not be the case if they had just met casually in the staff-room in the usual manner. T1 said: "I also found that I created friendships." In general education research novice teacher groups have reported a sense of belonging in such groups when they meet regularly, because as a member of the group they can share with others and discover they face similar issues and challenges, and as a result feel less isolation because they have the support of the group (Schlechty, 1984).

This was also true for the three novice ESL teachers in the reflection group discussed here. Through group membership and interactions all three teachers reported the benefits of collaboration as they shared experiences through meaningful discussions. In fact, we in the TESOL profession desire our students to display similar collaboration in our classrooms. As Redman (2006: 59) has observed:

> Good teachers work together. To be successful in today's world, teachers need to rid themselves of the mythical sense of classroom as kingdom. That was, for many years, an accepted part of the teaching profession. Teachers need to reach out and become collaborators,

supporters of one another and of the school as a whole. We need to develop skills of teacher leaders to end the isolation that can stunt professional learning and development. Good teachers know that teaching is no longer a lonely job.

In summary I would suggest that as a result of meeting regularly in a teacher reflection group all three novice ESL teachers benefited in the following manner; they were able to:

- Take responsibility for their learning and development.
- Combat isolation of the classroom and the novice year of teaching.
- Gain a better understanding of their teaching.
- Learn from others by listening to others' perspectives so that they could gain new knowledge and understanding about their practice.
- Give and receive encouragement and support.
- Reduce stress.
- Prepare for the future challenges.

Thus, the results reported on in this book suggest that novice teacher reflection groups can be used to combat the isolation many novice teachers report, and help them make a smoother transition from the teacher education program to their first year as ESL teachers.

## Reflective Break

- Comment on each of the five most common concerns of new teachers, as stated by Veenman (1984) from a review of 83 studies as follows:
  - o classroom discipline;
  - o motivating students;
  - o dealing with individual differences among students;
  - o assessment of student work;
  - o relationships with parents.
- Examine the benefits of meeting in a group above and comment on each.

# The Way Forward: Critical Components of Novice Teacher Reflection Groups

There are many characteristics in themselves that are important for the success of novice teacher reflection groups, but two of the most important that need attention are support from the school and the role of the facilitator. Without these I would suggest that novice teachers may not be able to continue reflecting for long, even if they are determined to have such a group. The novice teacher reflection group in this book was an anomaly of sorts because the group had no contacts with the school setting in which the novice teachers were placed. It happened by chance, with the facilitator looking for such a group of novice ESL teachers so he could learn more about their experiences, and the three novice teachers in search of opportunities to reflect. Of course, novice teachers can form similar groups in their schools but I would say this is the exception rather than the rule.

In addition, some kind of support from the administration would be essential for novice teachers to be able to form or join such a group. The administration could on the opening day of the school year inform all their novice teachers that such groups are available and welcomed in their school and that participation is voluntary and with no evaluations if they do decide to participate. They should be informed that they will gain valuable support from all in the school and as such will feel welcome to that community, but that they will not be evaluated as teachers in any way during their participation in the group. Novice teachers should also be informed that they will be treated like as such and given a reduced workload and duties so that they have the time to make their transition a success. In many other professions, such as baseball, the military and so on, newcomers are given such time to make a transition. As Turow (1977: 9) has noted:

> In baseball, it's the rookie year. In the Navy, it is boot camp. In many walks of life there is a similar time in trial and initiation, a period when newcomers are forced to be the victims of their own ineptness and when they must somehow master the basic skills of the profession in order to survive.

The next important issue is the choice of facilitator for the group. This person could come from within the school, such as an experienced teacher. I say "experienced" in the sense that we should also consider the knowledge of this facilitator because he or she will have to act in the role of a "knowledgeable other" as he or she facilitates the reflective process. As such the facilitator should have sufficient content knowledge and pedagogical knowledge to be able to make connections and clarifications as the group discussions develop, as well as knowledge of the reflective practice process. It would also be best if the facilitator had some kind of training in problem-solving and group discussions.

It would be good if this was a paid position (called *reflective coach*) but I am not sure how many schools would want to invest the time and money. However, for sure it should be a voluntary position and it should be clear that the facilitator will not be evaluating any of the novice teachers within the group, as participation is completely confidential: what is said in the group, stays in the group unless all members give their consent to speak outside the group setting. The facilitator will be responsible for setting up the group meetings and to keep the group going throughout the semester. The facilitator can use the same overall framework as used by the group in this book, and negotiate with group members such issues as how to create opportunities for reflection, negotiate ground rules, make provisions for time and build trust. Having acted as the facilitator of the group reported on here, I would suggest that the choice of facilitator is a crucial component of novice teacher reflection groups if they are to be successful.

## Reflective Break

- How can the administration better support novice teachers in their first year?
- How important is the group facilitator for novice teacher reflection groups?
- Chapter 2 outlined the core elements of the novice ESL teacher reflection group followed in this study: create opportunities for reflection, negotiate ground rules, make provisions for time and build trust. Use this same framework and consider the questions below to help guide you to form your own novice teacher reflection group (see Farrell, 2014, for more details on each of these):
  - *Type of Group*: Choose from three main types of teacher reflection groups (not only confined to the school you are in but maybe spanning several schools or school districts as well as other organizations):
    - a. Peer groups set up within the school (as was the case reported on in this book);
    - b. Teacher groups set up at the district level;
    - c. District-level groups, and virtual groups that can be formed anywhere.

o *Forming the Group*: Make sure each member feels safe, and connected within the group. How will you accomplish this and build
trust? Will you have a formal agreement on confidentiality about
what is discussed in the group?

o *Group Roles*: Who will be leader? Will the group have a facilitator
and, if so, what will the role of the facilitator be? Will a different
member be responsible for leading the discussion each week?

o *Discussion Topics*: Groups may want to first brainstorm together
on a theme or topic and then narrow it down by identifying specific questions to explore each week. This narrowing down of a
topic allows participants to focus their attention on issues that
have personal meaning for them.

o *Sustaining the Group*: In order to sustain any teacher reflection
group each member must be committed to the group. How
often will you meet?

o *Evaluating the Group*: After a teacher reflection group concludes
its period of reflection it is important that all group participants
evaluate the influences of the group on their personal and professional growth so that they can have some closure. How will you
do this?

## Limitations

In the opening chapter I pointed out one important limitation of not reporting
details of the personal identities of the three novice ESL teachers in order to protect their identities. As a result I realize that some may suggest that it is difficult to
generalize from this case study of just three novice ESL teachers in Canada because
every novice teacher will have a different experience in a different context. Indeed,
such a small sample size does not represent any total population. I explained in
chapter 1 why I wanted to protect their identities, and that the small sample size
was intended to allow for careful examination of how a novice teacher reflection
group can support other novice ESL teachers who want to reflect on their work.
However, it should also be noted that because of the in-depth first-year study
and work-intensive nature of this type of analysis, it is hard to undertake larger
databases.

Another limitation is that self-reports by the three novice ESL teachers could
be subject to memory, sensitivity to a particular topic, knowledge of a topic and

even sensitivity to other group members including this facilitator. This is another inherent problem in such type of research but, as noted above, all of the participants reported that they had a positive experience in the novice teacher reflection group.

I am well aware that the results of this case study may not provide the basis for prescription for all novice language teachers wishing to engage in reflective practice in a group during their first year; however, much of what is described and discussed in this book may have relevance for an individual novice ESL teacher's practice and context, as well as for teacher education programs and administrators who are interested in helping novice teachers through their first year. Further similar research should be carried out with novice teacher reflection groups in different contexts, and compared with the findings of this group. Indeed, further research could also compare the experiences of those novice teachers who choose to participate in such reflection groups with those who opt not to participate, to see if this has any impact on teacher retention. What is clear—however many limitations there are to the research in this book—is that teacher education programs could better prepare their novice teachers for the anticipated challenges and struggles they will inevitably encounter in their first year. Teacher educators could get more information themselves about these challenges and struggles by encouraging their learner-teachers to document their experiences in a journal. This information could be fed back into the teacher education program so that other novice language teachers could benefit from knowledge of their struggles. It is time now for the teaching profession to stop eating its young!

## Conclusion

This final chapter has suggested that, in addition to training novice teachers in the concept of reflective practice during their teacher education program, they should be enabled to continue this practice in their first year in a novice teacher reflection group. Such reflection groups are seen as a community of practice where teachers can combat the feelings of isolation, of having been left alone to sink or swim during their first year of teaching. These groups become especially important when schools for whatever reason do not have formal induction programs, nor mentors appointed to guide novice teachers. Thus the combination of reflective practice during teacher education programs (as discussed in chapter 9) and novice teacher reflection groups during the first year (as outlined in this chapter) can better help novice teachers make a smooth and successful transition into their new career as professionally qualified ESL teachers.

# References


Acheson, K.A., & Gall, M.D. (1987). *Techniques in the Clinical Supervision of Teachers: Preservice and Inservice Applications*. New York: Longman.

Achugar, M. (2009). Constructing a bilingual professional identity in a graduate classroom. *Journal of Language Identity Education*, 8, 2/3: 65–87.

Baecher, L. (2012). Feedback from the field: What novice preK-12 ESL teachers want to tell TESOL teacher educators. *TESOL Quarterly*, 46, 3: 578–88.

Bailey, K., Bergthold, B., Braunstein, B., Fleischman, N., Holbrook, M., Tuman, J., Waissbluth, X., & Zambo, L. 1996. The language learner's autobiography: Examining the "apprenticeship of observation." In D. Freeman & J. Richards (eds.), *Teacher Learning in Language Teaching* (pp. 11–29). Cambridge: Cambridge University Press.

Basturkmen, H. (2012). Review of research into the correspondence between language teachers' stated beliefs and practices, *System*, 40: 282–95.

Beaumont, M. & O'Brien, T. (2000). *Collaborative Research in Second Language Education*. Stoke-on-Trent: Trentham Books.

Belmonte, D. (2006). *Teaching on Solid Ground: Nuance, Challenge, and Technique for the Emerging Teacher*. Thousand Oaks, CA: Corwin Press.

Bogdan, R.C., & Biklen, S.K. (1982). *Qualitative Research for Education: An Introduction to Theory and Methods*. Boston: Allyn & Bacon.

Borg, S. (2003). Teacher cognition in language teaching: A review of research on what language teachers think, know, believe, and do. *Language Teaching*, 36: 81–109.

Brandt, S.L. (2005). A life preserver for the "sink or swim" years: An investigation of new teacher obstacles and the impact of a peer support group. Dissertation Abstracts International, 3443A (UMI No. 3201434).

Britzman, D.P. (1991). *Practice Makes Practice: A Critical Study of Learning to Teach*. Albany, NY: State University of New York Press.

Brookfield, S. (1990). *The Skilful Teacher*. San Francisco, CA: Jossey Bass.

Brouwer, N., & Korthagen, F. (2005) Can teacher education make a difference? *American Educational Research Journal*, 42, 1: 153–224.

Bullough, R.V. (1997). Practicing theory and theorizing practice in teacher education. In J. Loughran & T. Russell (eds.), *Teaching about Teaching* (pp. 13–31). London: Falmer Press.

Burns, A., & Richards, J.C. (eds). (2009). *The Cambridge Guide to Second Language Teacher Education*. New York: Cambridge University Press.

Calderhead, J. (1992). Induction: A research perspective on the professional growth of the newly qualified teacher. In J. Calderhead & J. Lambert (eds.), *The Induction of Newly Appointed Teachers* (pp. 5–21). General Teaching Council for England and Wales.

Cejda, B.D. (1997). An examination of transfer shock in academic disciplines. *Community College Journal of Research and Practice*, 21: 279–88.

Clair, N. (1998). Teacher study groups: persistent questions in a promising approach. *TESOL Quarterly*, 32: 465–92.

Cogan, M. (1973). *Clinical Supervision*. Boston, MA: Houghton Mifflin.

Cohen, J.L. (2008). "That's not treating you as a professional": Teachers constructing complex professional identities through talk. *Teachers and Teaching: Theory and Practice*, 14, 2: 79–93.

Corcoran, E. (1981). Transition shock: The beginning teacher's paradox. *Journal of Teacher Education*, 32, 3: 19–23.

Crow, J., & Smith, L. (2005). Co-teaching in higher education: Reflective conversations on shared experience as continued professional development for lecturers and health and social care students. *Reflective Practice*, 6, 4: 491–506.

Dellar, G. (1990). The needs of novice teachers: A case study. In J. Roberts (ed.), *CALS Workpapers: Initial Training and the First Year in School* (pp. 62–77). Reading: Centre for Applied Language Studies, University of Reading.

Faez, F., & Valeo, A. (2012). TESOL teacher education: Novice teachers' perceptions of their preparedness and efficacy in the classroom. *TESOL Quarterly*, 46, 3: 450–71.

Farrell, T.S.C. (1999). The reflective assignment: Unlocking preservice teachers' prior beliefs. *RELC Journal*, 30, 2: 1–17.

Farrell, T.S.C. (2003). Learning to teach English language during the first year: Personal influences and challenges. *Teaching and Teacher Education*, 19: 95–111.

Farrell, T.S.C. (2004a). *Reflective Practice in Action*. Thousand Oaks, CA: Corwin Press.

Farrell, T.S.C. (2004b). *Reflecting on Classroom Communication in Asia*. Singapore: Longman.

Farrell, T.S.C. (2006). The first year of language teaching: Imposing order. *System*, 34, 2: 211–21.

Farrell, T.S.C. (2007). *Reflective Language Teaching: From Research to Practice*. London: Continuum Press.

Farrell, T.S.C. (ed.). (2008). *Novice Language Teachers: Insights and Perspectives for the First Year*. London: Equinox.

Farrell, T.S.C. (2009). The novice teacher. In A. Burns & J.C. Richards (eds.), *The Cambridge Guide to Second Language Teacher Education* (pp. 182–9). New York: Cambridge University Press.

Farrell, T.S.C. (2012a). Novice-service language teacher development: Bridging the gap between preservice and in-service education and development. *TESOL Quarterly*, 46, 3: 435–49.

Farrell, T.S.C. (2012b). *Reflective Writing for Language Teachers*. London: Equinox.

Farrell, T.S.C. (2014). *Reflective Practice in ESL Teacher Development Groups: From Practices to Principles*. Basingstoke: Palgrave Macmillan.

Farrell, T.S.C. (2015a). *Promoting Teacher Reflection in Second Language Education: A Framework for TESOL Professionals*. New York: Routledge.

Farrell, T.S.C. (ed.). (2015b). *International Perspectives on English Language Teacher Education: Innovations from the Field*. Basingstoke: Palgrave Macmillan.

Farrell, T.S.C., & Lim. P. (2005). Grammar teaching: A case study of teachers' beliefs and classroom practices. *TESL-EJ* (September).

Feiman-Nemser, S. (2003). What new teachers need to learn. *Educational Leadership*, 60, 8: 25–30.

Flynn, S.P., & Hekelman, F.P. (1993). Reality shock: A case study in the socialization of new residents. *Family Medicine*, 25: 633–6.

Franzak, J.K. (2002). Developing a teacher identity: The impact of critical friends practice on the student teacher. *English Education*, 34, 4: 258–81.

Freeman, D. (1994). Knowing into doing: Teacher education and the problem of transfer. In D. Li, D. Mahony and J.C. Richards (eds.), *Exploring Second Language Teacher Development* (pp. 1–20). Hong Kong: City University Press.

Fuller, F.F., & Brown, O.H. (1975). Becoming a teacher. In K. Ryan (ed.), *Teacher Education: The Seventy-fourth Yearbook of the National Society for the Study of Education* (pp. 25–51). Chicago: National Society for the Study of Education.

Glesne, C., & Peshkin, A. (1992). *Becoming Qualitative Researchers: An Introduction*. New York: Longman.

Goetz, J., & LeCompte, M. (1984). *Ethnography and Qualitative Design in Educational Research*. San Diego: Academic Press.

Grasha, A.F. 1996. *Teaching with Style: A Practical Guide to Enhancing Learning by Understanding Teaching and Learning Styles*. Pittsburgh: Alliance Publishers.

Halford, J. (1998). Easing the way for new teachers. *Educational Leadership*, 55, 5: 33–6.

Hammond Stoughton, E. (2007). "How will I get them to behave?" Pre service teachers reflect on classroom management. *Teaching and Teacher Education*, 23, 7: 1024–37.

Head, K., & Taylor, P. (1997). *Readings in Teacher Development*. London: Heinemann.

Hiebert, J., Gallimore, R., & Stigler, J.W. (2002). A knowledge base for the teaching profession: What would it look like and how can we get one? *Educational Researcher*, 31, 5: 3–15.

Huling, L., Resta, V., & Yeargain, P. (2012). Supporting and retaining novice teachers. *Kappa Delta Pi Record*, 48, 3: 140–3.

Humaira, A., & Rarieya, J.F.A., 2008. Teacher development through reflective conversations—possibilities and tensions: A Pakistan case. *Reflective Practice*, 9: 269–79

Ingersoll, R. (2001). Teacher turnover and teacher shortages: An organizational analysis. *American Educational Research Journal*, 38, 3: 499–535.

Ingersoll, R.M., & Smith, T.M. (2003). The wrong solution to the teacher shortage. *Educational Leadership*, 60, 8: 30–3.

Jay, J.K., & Johnson, K.L. (2002). Capturing complexity: A typology of reflective practice for teacher education. *Teaching and Teacher Education*, 18: 73–85.

Johnson, K.E. (1992). Learning to teach: Instructional actions and decisions of preservice ESL teachers. *TESOL Quarterly*, 26: 507–35.

Johnson, K.E. (1996). The vision versus the reality: The tensions of the TESOL practicum. In D. Freeman & J. Richards (eds.), *Teacher Learning in Language Teaching* (pp. 30–49). New York: Cambridge University Press.

Johnson, K.E. (2009). *Second Language Teacher Education: A Sociocultural Perspective.* New York: Routledge.

Joiner, S., & Edwards, J. (2008). Novice teachers: Where are they going and why don't they stay? *Journal of Cross-Disciplinary Perspectives in Education*, 1, 1: 36–43.

Kaufmann, R., & Ring, M. (2011). Pathways to leadership and professional development: Inspiring novice special educators. *Teaching Exceptional Children*, 43, 5: 52–60.

Kelchtermans, G., & Ballet, K. (2002). The micropolitics of teacher induction: A narrative-biographical study on teacher socialisation. *Teaching and Teacher Education*, 18: 105–20.

Lewis, R., Romi, S., Qui, X., & Katz, Y.J. (2005). Teachers' classroom discipline and student misbehaviour in Australia, China and Israel. *Teaching and Teacher Education*, 21: 729–41.

Lincoln, Y.S., & Guba, E.G. (1985). *Naturalistic Inquiry.* Beverly Hills: Sage.

Loughran, J., Brown, J., & Doecke, B. (2001). Continuities and discontinuities: The transition from pre-service to first year teaching. *Teachers and Teaching: Theory and Practice*, 7, 1: 7–23.

Mann, S. (2005). The language teacher's development. *Language Teaching*, 38: 103–18.

Mattheoudakis, K.M. (2007). Tracking changes in pre-service EFL teacher beliefs in Greece: A longitudinal study. *Teaching and Teacher Education*, 23: 1272–88.

McDermott, R., & Roth, D. (1978). The social organization of behavior: Interactional approaches. *Annual Review of Anthropology*, 7: 321–45.

Merrett, F., & Wheldall, K. (1993). How do teachers learn to manage classroom behaviour? A study of teachers' opinions about their initial training with special reference to classroom behaviour management. *Educational Studies*, 19: 91–106.

Merriam, S.B. (1988). *Case Study Research in Education: A Qualitative Approach.* San Francisco: Jossey-Bass.

Miller, J. (2009). Teacher identity. In A. Burns & J.C. Richards (eds.), *The Cambridge Guide to Second Language Teacher Education* (pp. 172–81). New York: Cambridge University Press.

Moreno, J.L. (1953). *Who Shall Survive?* Beacon, NY: Beacon House.

O'Connor, I., & Dalgleish, L. (1986). Cautionary tales from beginning practitioners: The fate of personal models of social work in beginning practice. *British Journal of Social Work*, 16: 431–47.

O'Neill, S.C., & Stephenson, J. (2014). Evidence-based classroom and behaviour management content in Australian pre-service primary teachers' coursework: Wherefore art thou? *Australian Journal of Teacher Education*, 39, 4: 1–22.

Osterman, K., & Kottkamp, R. (2004). *Reflective Practice for Educators.* Thousand Oaks, CA: Corwin Press.

Peterson, B.E., & Williams, S.R. (1998). Mentoring beginning teachers. *The Mathematics Teacher*, 91: 730–4.

Phillips, D. (1989). *Pilot Study of the Career Paths of EFL Teachers*. London: Centre for British Teachers.

Redman, P.D. (2006). *Don't Smile until December and Other Myths about Classroom Teaching*. Thousand Oaks, CA: Corwin Press.

Reid, J. (2011). A practice turn for teacher education? *Asia-Pacific Journal of Teacher Education*, 39, 4: 293–310.

Richards, J.C. (1998). *Beyond Training*. New York: Cambridge University Press.

Richards, J.C., & Farrell, T.S.C (2005). *Professional Development for Language Teachers*. New York: Cambridge University Press.

Richards, J.C. & Farrell, T.S.C. (2011). *Teaching Practice: A Reflective Approach*. New York: Cambridge University Press.

Richards, J.C., & Lockhart, C. (1994). *Reflective Teaching*. New York: Cambridge University Press.

Richards, K. (2003). *Qualitative Inquiry in TESOL*. Basingstoke: Palgrave Macmillan.

Riordan, S., & Goodman, S. (2007). Managing reality shock: Expectations versus experiences of graduate engineers. *SA Journal of Industrial Psychology*, 33: 67–73.

Roberts, J. (1998). *Language Teacher Education*. London: Arnold.

Rogers, D.L., and Babinski, L.M. (2002) *From Isolation to Conversation: Supporting New Teachers' Development*. Albany, NY: State University of New York Press.

Saracho, O.N. (2000). A framework for effective classroom teaching. In R.J. Riding & S.G. Rayner (eds.), *International Perspectives on Individual Differences, Volume 1: Cognitive Styles* (pp. 297–314). Stamford, CT: Ablex Publishing.

Schlechty, P.C. (1984). *Restructuring the Teaching Occupation: A Proposal*. Washington, DC: American Educational Research Association.

Schön, D.A. (1983). *The Reflective Practitioner: How Professionals Think in Action*. New York: Basic Books.

Schultz, B.G. (1989). *Communicating in a Small Group: Theory and Practice*. New York: Harper Collins.

Senior, R. (2006). *The Experience of Language Teaching*. New York: Cambridge University Press.

Shanker, A. (1990). Restructuring the teaching profession and our schools. In D. Dill (ed.), *What Teachers Need to Know: The Knowledge, Skills, and Values Essential to Good Teaching* (1st ed., pp. 209–21). San Francisco: Jossey-Bass.

Shin, S. (2012). "It cannot be done alone": The socialization of novice English teachers in South Korea. *TESOL Quarterly*, 46, 3: 542–67.

Shulman, L. (1992). Ways of seeing, ways of knowing, ways of teaching, ways of learning about teaching. *Journal of Curriculum Studies*, 28: 393–6.

Smith, T.M., & Ingersoll, R. (2004). What are the effects of induction and mentoring on beginning teacher turnover? *American Education Research Journal*, 41, 3: 681–714.

So, W.M.M., and Watkins, D.A. (2005). From beginning teacher education to professional teaching: A study of the thinking of Hong Kong primary science teachers. *Teaching and Teacher Education*, 21: 525–41.

Stake, R. (1995). *The Art of Case Study Research*. Beverly Hills, CA: Sage.

Tafa, E.M. (2004). Teacher socialisation: A critical qualitative analysis of the teaching methods of seven new teachers in Botswana junior secondary schools. *International Journal of Educational Development*, 24: 757–8.

Tarone, E., & Allwright, D. (2005). Second language teacher learning and student second language learning: Shaping the knowledge base. In D.J. Tedick (ed.), *Second Language Teacher Education* (pp. 5–23). Mahwah, NJ: Lawrence Erlbaum.

Theil, T. (1999). Reflections on critical incidents. *Prospect*, 14, 1: 44–52.

Tsui, A. (2003). *Understanding Expertise in Teaching: Case Studies of ESL Teachers*. New York: Cambridge University Press.

Turow, S. (1977). *One L: The Turbulent True Story of a First Year at Harvard Law School*. New York: G.P. Putnam's Sons.

U.S. Department of Education. (2000). *Eliminating Barriers to Improving Teaching*. Washington, DC: National Center for Education Statistics.

Varah, L.J., Theune, W.S., & Parker, L. (1986). Beginning teachers: sink or swim? *Journal of Teacher Education*, 37: 30–3.

Varghese, M., Morgan, B., Johnston, B., & Johnson, K. (2005). Theorizing language teacher identity: Three perspectives and beyond. *Journal of Language, Identity, and Education*, 4, 1: 21–44.

Veenman, S. (1984). Perceived problems of beginning teachers. *Review of Educational Research*, 54: 143–78.

Walkington, J. (2005). Becoming a teacher; Encouraging development of teacher identity through reflective practice. *Asia-Pacific Journal of Teacher Education*, 33, 1: 53–64.

Wallace, M. (1998). *Action Research for Language Teachers*. Cambridge: Cambridge University Press.

Wenger, E. (1998). *Communities of Practice: Learning, Meaning, and Identity*. New York: Cambridge University Press.

Wideen, M., Mayer-Smith, J., & Moon, B. (1998). A critical analysis of the research on learning to teach: Making the case for the ecological perspective on inquiry. *Review of Educational Research*, 68: 130–78.

Woods, D. (1996). *Teacher Cognition in Language Teaching*. Cambridge: Cambridge University Press.

Wright, T. (2010). Second language teacher education: Review of recent research on practice. *Language Teaching*, 43, 3: 259–96.

# Index

CPSIA information can be obtained
at www.ICGtesting.com
Printed in the USA
JSHW072031230223
38149JS00002B/39